Abstracts
from
The North Carolina Gazette
of
New Bern, North Carolina
- 1751-1759 *and* 1768-1790 -

(Volume #1)

Compiled By:
Raymond Parker Fouts

Southern Historical Press, Inc.
Greenville, South Carolina

This volume was reproduced
from a personal copy located in
the Publishers private library

Please direct all correspondence and book orders to:
SOUTHERN HISTORICAL PRESS, Inc.
PO Box 1267
Greenville, SC   29602-1267

PREFACE

These abstracts were made from microfilm of the
original newspapers, obtained from the North Carolina
State Archives at Raleigh, North Carolina. Information
concerning dates and sources is included at the beginning
of each year. All issues located are included, though
nothing may have been abstracted from them.

Advertisements are recorded only from the first
issue in which they appear. Spelling and punctuation
have been followed as closely as possible.

Each item has been assigned a number that is enclosed
within parentheses. The name index and location index
refer to these numbers.

TABLE OF CONTENTS

Text 1-98

Index 99-114

Location Index 115-118

ABSTRACTS FROM THE NORTH CAROLINA GAZETTE

OF NEW BERN, NORTH CAROLINA

1751-1759 and 1768-1790

1751 - All issues missing except for the following from Department
of Archives and History-November 15.

November 15, 1751.
THE NOT$^{\underline{H}}$ CAROLINA GAZETTE (Numb. 15.)
With the freshest Advices, Foreign and Domestic.
All Persons may be supplied with this Paper, at Four Shillings,
Proclamation Money, per Quarter, by James DAVIS, at the Printing-
Office in Newbern; where all Manner of Printing-Work, ___ Book-
Binding, is done reasonably. Advertisements of a moderate Length,
are inserted for Three Shillings the first Week, and Two Shillings
for every Week after.

(1) July 31. Mr. William CURTIS, Commander of the Goodwill Merchant Ship, now in the River, who left Cape Francois June 4 where
he had been eight Months, in that Time saw 1500 English Sailors in
the French Service, on board their Merchant Ships; and says, that
he took an Account of 480 Sail that went out of that Port for France,
all richly laden.

(2) Advertisements. To be Sold, by the Subscriber, several Tracts
of Land; and Town-Lots, viz. A Plantation, known by the name of
Lilleput, within two Miles of Brunswick containing 1280 Acres,
fronting on the River, about three Quarters of a Mile, and on a
Creek near three Miles, adjoining the River and Creek; there is at
least 200 Acr__ of Marsh, and Swamp, very good Rice Land, and a very
good Brick Dwelling-house, and other convenient Out-houses on said
Land. Also, another Tract of Land, at Rockey-Point, containing 640
Acres, known by the name of Spring-Field, fronting on the North-East
River..Rice Land..about 150 Acres.. The Remainder of the said Land
..good..for Corn, Indigo, &c..a very good Brick barn, 42 Feet by 23,
a Dwelling-house, and other Out-houses. Also, another Tract of Land
containing 640 Acres, upon Maxwell's Swamp, on the North-East River,
and lies on both Sides of the Road, leading from Rock-fish Creek,
to Soracte. Maxwell's Swamp runs through the middle of it... Also,
another Tract of Land, on New-River, near Everard's Ferry, containing 640 Acres... Also, another Tract of Land, containing 215 Acres,
joining to the Town of Newbern... Also, a front Lot of Land in the
North End of Brunswick, joining on the North Side of the Land where
Mr. CHALKHILL now liveth. Also, a Lot of Land in Wilmington, No. 34,

1

(2) (Cont.) joining to the North Side of Mr. James CAMPBELL's.
Any Person inclined to purchase any of the said Tracts of Land or
Town Lots, may treat with the Subscriber. Sarah ALLEN.

(3) Ran away from the Subscriber, a Negroe Fellow, named FRANK;..
Whoever brings him to me, shall have Thirteen Shillings and Four
Pence, Proclamation Money, Reward, besides the Country Allowance,
paid by Samuel JOHNSTON.

(4) To be Sold, by the Subscriber, living in Norfolk, in Virginia,
by Wholesale or Retail. Simple Drugs of all sorts, Chymical and
Galenical Medicines..Spices, Oils, Pickles,..Prunes, Raisins, Cur-
rants, Figgs, Sago, Turlington's Balsam, Stoughton's, Dassey's (or
Daffey's), and Squire's Elixirs, Bateman's Drops, Lockier's and Anderson's Pills, Coral and Annocine (?) Necklaces, British Rock Oil
.. ____habald CAMPBELL.

Newbern: Printed __ James DAVIS, at the Printing-Office, near the
Church.

1752 - All issues missing except for the following from Department
of Archives and History-March 6, 13.

March 6. (Masthead missing on this issue; date is handwritten.)

(5) London, Oct. 4. There is lately arrived in Town from the East-
Indies, but last from Lisbon, a Man of the most surprizing unaccount-
able Genius..an Italian, and a Native of Civita Vecchia, named Sig-
nore Andero Grimalde VOLANTE, aged about Fifty, of a middle Stature,
in Holy Orders of the College of Jesus..after fourteen Years great
Labour and Expence has compleated one of the most astonishing and
compleatest Pieces of Mechanism, the World ever yet beheld. It is
a Case of a most curious Texture and Workmanship, which, by the
Help of Clockwork, is made to amount in the Air, and to proceed with
that Rapidity of Force and Swiftness, as to be able to travel at the
Rate of seven Leagues an Hour. It is in the shape of a great Bird..
whose Wings, from Tip to Tip, is twenty two Feet; the Body is composed of Pieces of Cork, curiously held together by Joints of Wire,
covered with Vellum and Feathers; the Wings of Cat gutt and Whale
bone Springs, and covered with the same, and folds up in three Joints
each. In the Body of the Machine is contained thirty Wheels, of
peculiar Make, with two Rollers, or Barrels of Brass, and small
Chains which alternately wind off from each other a counterpoize
Weight, and by the Help of six Brass Tubes, that slide in Groves,
with Partitions in them, and loaded with a certain Quantity of
Quicksilver, the Machine is by help of the Artist, kept in due Equi-
librium and Ballance; and by the Friction of a Steel Wheel, properly
tempered, and a large surprizing Magnet, the whole is kept in regular progressive Motion, unless the Temperature of Winds and Weather
prevents, for he can no more fly in a Calm than he can in a Storm.
This wonderful Machine is guided and directed by a Tail seven Feet
long, which is fastened by Leather Straps to his Knees and Ancles;
and by the expanding his Legs, either..Right or Left, he moves the
Whole which way he chuses..the Machine flies, (which is but three
hours) and then the Wings gradually closes, and he of Course lights

(5) (Cont.) gently on his Feet, when he winds up the Clockwork,
and sets himself again on the Wing...

(6) Philadelphia, December 31. By Cape Flower, from South-Carolina
there is Advice, that the Rev. Mr. George WHITEFIELD designs to sail
for this Place early in the Spring.

(7) Boston, October 21. Extract from the Votes of the Honourable
House of Representatives. Martis 8 Die Octobris, A. D. 1751. James
MINOS, Esq. brought down the Report of the Committee of both Houses
appointed the third Instant, relating to the Western Tribes of
Indians, &c....

March 13, 1752. (Numb. 32.)

(8) Custom-house, Port-Beaufort, Entered inwards. March. Sloop
Three Brothers, Nathaniel SCOT, Master, Boston. Shallop Charming
Sally, John FREDWEL, Master, from Virginia. Snow Industry, Thomas
COLLINSON, Master, from Lancaster. Sloop Ranger, Ebenezer WHITE,
Master, from Rhode-Island. Sloop Success, William CORD, Master,
from Virginia. Sloop Phaenix, Mathew KING, Master, from Rhode-
Island. Sloop Sugar Box, Robert BRIDGES, Master, from Ditto.

    Clear'd out. March. Sloop Susanna, Zephaniah PINKHAM, for
Boston. Sloop Abigal, Thomas CHITTENDEN, Master, for Ditto. Sloop
Sally, Seth CLARK, Master, for Boston. Sloop Freetown, Cary GODBY,
Master, for Rhode-Island.

(9) Advertisements. Ran away from the Subscribers, on Roanoke
River, a Negro Fellow, named Thomas BOMAN, a very good Black-Smith,
near six Feet high,..he can read, write and cypher.. Whoever will
apprehand..him, so that the Owners may get him, shall be paid..12
Pistoles, besides what the Law allows... Robert WEST, sen., Robert
WEST, jun.

1753 - All issues missing except for the following from Department
of Archives and History-July 7, 1 copy-undated.

July 7, 1753.

(10) Newbern, July 7. __ hear from Eden-House, the Seat of our
late Governor, That __ Days since the said House was, by some Accident, entirely ____med by Fire; but as we don't know the Particulars
we must ____ _ur Readers to our next.

(11) North-Carolina. By the Honourable Matthew __AN, Esq; President and Commander in Chief, in and over his Majesty's Province of
North-Carolina. A Proclamation. Whereas..sundry Persons, under
Colour and Pretence of Authority from his Majesty's Officers, in the
Province of South-Carolina, have come into the County of Anson within this Province, and have surveyed Lands.. And whereas, such illegal Proceedings tend manifestly to disturb the Peace, raise Doubts
about the Property, and retard the Settlement of the said County of
Anson, which is a Frontier to the Indians..Issue this my Proclamation..strictly requiring and commanding his Majesty's Officers..to

3

(11) (Cont.) apprehend..every such Offender... Given under my Hand, and the Great Seal of the said Province, at Wilmington, the 10th Day of May, in the XXVI Year of his Majesty's Reign, Anno Domini 1753. Matt. ROWAN. By his Honour's Command. Ja. MURRAY, Sec.

(12) Newbern, June 16, 1753. On Wednesday Night last, broke out of Goal in this Town, two Servant Men, belonging to Mr. John MITCHELSON, of Virginia, viz. Benjamin BOND, a Miller, aged about 40, of a middle Stature, much pitted with the Small-Pox, of a ruddy Complexion. Paul PRICE, a Baker, aged about 19 or 20, a smooth-fac'd well looking Lad... Whoever delivers the said Servants to me in Newbern, shall have Forty Shillings Reward. Southy REW, Sheriff.

(13) Wilmington, June 23, 1753. All persons who are indebted to DAVIES and MACKENZIE, are desired to come and settle their respective Accompts by the last of August... William MACKENZIE.

(14) June 25, 1753. Ran away from the Subscriber, in Johnston County..a Negroe Fellow named SAM,..about 5 Feet 4 Inches high: He has been taken up lately, and committed to Newbern Goal, from which he was delivered to Mr. John SMITH, in order to be carried to his Master; but broke out of Custody of..Smith, near the South-West Bridge.. Twenty Five Shillings Reward, besides what the Law allows. John DICKSON.

__wbern: Printed by James DAVIS, at the Printing-Office in Front-Street.

Undated Copy-Illegible.

1754-1755-1756-No issues located.

1757 - All issues missing except for the following-April 15.
Note: Filmed from photostats, in the Department of Archives and History, from the British Public Records Office in London, England.

Friday, April 15, 1757. (Numb. 103.)

(15) North-Carolina, ss. By his Excellency Arthur DOBBS, Esq., His Majesty's Captain-General, Governor, and Commander in Chief, in and over the said Province. A Proclamation, For the Meeting of the Assembly. Whereas on the present Emergency of Affairs..the several Members of the said Assembly are..directed to be,..and meet at Newbern, on Friday the Thirteenth Day of May next... Given under my Hand, and the Seal of the said Province, at Newbern, the 9th Day of April, 1757, and in the 30th Year of his Majesty's Reign. Arthur DOBBS. By his Excellency's Command, William POWEL, Dep. Secretary. God Save the King.

(16) Advertisements. Whoever have Patents for Land, granted either in Governor JOHNSTON's, or President RICE's Time, whether they are in the hands of the Subscriber, or lying in the Secretary's Office at Newbern, may, on speedy Application to me, obtain the same, paying the Fees due thereon. John RICE.

4

(17) To Be Sold Reasonably; Sundry Valuable Tracts of Land, lying
in the Counties of Craven, Johnston, Edgcombe, and Granville.
Robert BRINKLEY, Esq; has a Power to dispose of the Lands in Edgecombe and Granville.. Joseph CARR___(?) N. B. The Lands in Edgecombe and Granville were patented by Joseph ANDERSON, Esq;

(18) Newbern, April 8th, 1757. This is to inform the Public, that
the Courts of Chancery and Claims..are further prorogued to the 17th
Day of May next. Richard SPAIGHT, Secretary.

(19) To all Those concerned in making Pot-Ash. Notice is hereby
given by Mr. STEPHENS, that he intends to return, from Savannah in
Georgia, To Mrs. DAVIDSON's, at Poupon in South-Carolina, April 15,
Mr. TRUSTER's in Charles-Town, 18, Ferry at George Town, 24, Ferry
at Brunswick, North Carolina, 28, Mrs. MAC CORKALL's at Wilmington,
30, Mr. RICHARDSON's at Newbern, May 10, Mr. COUTANCH's at Bath,
15, Mrs. WALLACE's at Edenton, 17, Mr. JONES's at Suffolk, Virginia,
20, Ferry at Norfolk, 22, Ferry at Hampton, 23, Mr. HUNTER's at
Williamsburg, 25.

(20) Ran away from the Subscriber in Newbern, an Irish Servant
Woman, named Mary LAMBERT, a short, lusty, full faced Woman, very
fresh Complexion, wears her Hair down behind, which is very black,
and curls handsomely... Whoever brings the said Servant to me in
Newbern, shall have Forty Shillings Reward. James DAVIS.

(21) Thirty Pounds Reward. Ran away the 18th of February 1757 (?),
from on board the Sloop Phebe & Polly, Thomas REMER, Master, lying
in Smith's Creek in Neuse River, James ROSS, about 5 feet 5 inches
high..was brought from the North of Ireland, and lived in Maryland,
Philadelphia, and West New-Jersey, had Masters in all the aforesaid
Places, but made it a Practice of leaving them; sold to the Subscriber by Joseph BLOOMFIELD in New-York. Also, James J_ff_ry F___ S_LL
about 6 Feet High.. Isaac N_TIE (?), born in Maryland, about 5 Feet
6 Inches high, about 21 Years of Age... Solomon _____... Run away
also, from the said sloop.. Peter RIEBEUR (?), about 5 Feet 6 Inches
high.. he is a Frenchman, and speaks a little English. Anthony
C_BERRITT (?), about 5 Feet 4 Inches High,..swarthy complexion..is
a Spaniard, and speaks very little English.. Whoever apprehends
the said Runaways, and delivers them to the Subscriber, or the Sheriff of Craven County, shall have Five Pounds Reward for each, and
Twenty Shillings for the Canoe. Rip VAN DAM. N. B. They were
brought here by Captain TRIGG, from Providence, and have lain in Goa
some Time.

1758 - No issues located.

1759 - All issues missing except for the following from American
Antiquarian Society-October 18.

Thursday, October 18, 1759. (Numb. 200.)

(22) New-York. Sept. 10. The Albany Post, who arrived here last
Night, informs, That Gen. AMHERST, with his Army remained yet at
Crown-Point, all in good Health: That it was currently reported at

5

(22) (Cont.) Albany, that Brigadier Gen. GAGE had set out from
Oswego, with a large Body of his Army, in order to attack Oswegat-
chi, &c. That on Thursday last an Express from Boston went through
Albany, with Letters for General AMHERST, relating to the Situation
of Gen. WOLFE and his Army.

(23) New-York, Sept. 10. A few Months ago, died in Dutchess County,
in this Province, Mr. Jeremiah KANNEIF, aged 96 Years, whose wife
died about 3 Years since: They lived together in the Marriage State
71 Years and 9 Months!

(24) Extract of a Letter from Albany, Sept. 9, 1759. .. The Account Captain Robert STOBO gave of the Strength of Quebec when he
made his Escape from thence, is as follows...

(25) Charles-Town, Sept. 29. By Capt. WILSON from Philadelphia..
we have Papers to the 13th Instant, and Letters of the 18th, Which
contain the following Advices.. That Captain KENNEDY, of GAGE's
Light Infantry, with a few Indians, had undertaken to cross the
Country, with Dispatches to General WOLFE, and set off from Crown-
Point the 8th ult. That Lieutenant HUTCHENS, of ROGERS's Rangers,
had also gone on a like Errand, another Way.. That General STANWIX
had reached Pittsburgh..; Col. MERCER was gone to reconnoitre the
ruined Venango; and most of the French Inhabitants on the Ohio and
nearest Lakes, were determined to go down the Missisippi. Sunday
last arrived here two Vessels in 17 Days from Jamaica.. That Captain John MARKHAM, of the Ship Elizabeth, was arrived there from
Falmouth in Casco Bay.

(26) Newbern, October 18. On Friday last, an Express arrived here
from Charles Town on his Way to Virginia, with Dispatches from Governor LITTLETON to the Governor of Virginia; the Occasion of which
is said to be, the Cherokees taking up Arms in Favour of the French;
and that they are assembling in Bodies to make Depredations on our
Frontiers.

(27) Advertisements. Just imported in the St. Andrew, from London,
but last from Boston, and to be sold by Richard FARR, at Beaufort..
London Cordage, Ticklingburghs..Cloth..Sail Twine..Shirts..Jackets..
Drawers..White Cups and Saucers..Bowls, Mugs, Plates and Dishes..
Tortoise Shell Cups and Saucers, Teapots &c., Glasses..Loaf Sugar..
Powder.. N. B. ..: the said FARR intendeth to leave the Country
in 6 Weeks..all..that taketh large Quantities, shall have an Allow-
ance made.

(28) North Carolina, ss. Whereas thro' sundry Misfortunes we have
been unable to carry on our Business in the mercantile Way, and
sundry Judgments.. against us by..our Creditors..particularly by
Robert HARBIN, of the Town of Newbern..we have transferred and set
over.,.and delivered..to Robert HARBIN, all our Books of Accounts,
with whom all Persons indebted to us, are desired to pay their respective Debts: Hereby also giving Notice, That we shall make Application to the..Supreme Court..at Newbern in March next, that the
Benefit of the Act, in relation to insolvent Debtors, may be to us
extended.. Dated Newbern, October 4th, 1759. Richard WALKER,
Joseph FISHER.

1768 - All issues missing except for the following from American
Antiquarian Society-June 24. From Department of Archives and History
-July 21.

June 24, 1768. (Numb. 5.)

With the latest Advices, Foreign and Domestick.
Printed by James DAVIS, at the Post-Office in Newbern.

(29) Newbern, June 24. Custom-House, Port-Beaufort. Entered In-
wards. June 16. Schooner Poor Man's Friend, Robert SHORT, from
Philadelphia. Cleared Outwards. June 11. Sloop Diamond, Benjamin
CRANE, for St. Christopher's. 21. Sloop Polly, James BAZZEY, for
Philadelphia, do. Sloop Desire, Nath. BOWLES, for Boston. do. Sloop
Tryal, W. WOOLCUTT, for Barbadoes. 22. Sloop Dolphin, Robt. WEST-
COTE, for N. York. do. Snow Friendship, George RICHARDSON, for
Gibraltar.

(30) Advertisements. Newbern, June 24, 1768. The Subscriber having
been a great Sufferer by Persons trespassing on his Lands on Slocombs
Creek, and at Green Spring, near this Town, finds himself under the
Necessity of forbidding all Persons from hunting, shooting, or rang-
ing thereon on any Pretence; as he is determined to prosecute any
that shall be found offending herein. James DAVIS.

(31) June 24, 1768. Ran away from the Subscriber in Newbern, a
yellowish Fellow named WILL, about 45 Years of Age, very stout and
lusty... James DAVIS.

July 21, 1768. (Nothing transcribed.)

1769 - All issues missing except for the following-November 10.
Note: Filmed from photostats, in the Department of Archives & History, from the British Public Records Office in London, England.

Friday, November 10, 1769. (Number 73.)

(32) Newbern. To his excellency William TRYON, Esq. his majesty's
captain general, governor and commander in chief in and over the
province of North Carolina. The humble Address of his Majesty's
council of the Said province...

(33) On Saturday last, his Excellency the governor sent a message
to the house, desiring their attendance on him in the council chamber
... On Monday, the house came to the following Resolutions: On
Motion, Resolved, That if any public Officer shall exact illegal
fees..unduly oppress the people..shall receive the highest censure.
On Motion, Resolved, That all persons who oppose Sheriffs in the
due execution of their office shall be looked upon..as enemies to
their country, meriting its severest censures..and highest punishment.. In the house of assembly, 6th of Nov. 1769. J. GREEN, Jun.,
Clerk. The same day..his Excellency..was pleased to give his assent
to four bills viz... An Act for confirming the qualification of
Henry LOCKEY, Sheriff of Beaufort...

(34) Advertisements. To be Sold, on reasonable terms, for ready money, in Tyrell county, One thousand acres of land, with a saw mill, on the head of Gardner's creek..also, 100 acres of land, with a grist mill, about a mile from Roanoke river... John HARDISON. Nov. 10, 1769.

(35) Newbern, November 10. Last week, died at Halifax, in an advanced age, Mr. Stephen DEWEY; a gentleman of an unblemished character, and great abilities in his profession of the Law.

(36) Onslow county, Oct. 20, 1769. Taken up and conveyed to the county goal on New-River, four likely Negro Fellows... Lewis WILLIAMS, Sheriff.

(37) John OWENS, In the Brig. Peggy, is just arrived from London, with a fresh assortment of Goods, suitable for the season now opening at Robert WILLIAMS's ready money store... Newbern, October 27, 1769.

(38) Stray'd from Granville county..two Horses... James MACARTNEY. October 27, 1769.

(39) Rowan county, Oct. 13, 1769. Ran away from the subscriber on the third day of September last, three outlandish negroes, viz..a negro fellow named JACK, about 26 or 2_ years old, about 5 feet 6 inches high, well set, of a pleasant countenance..also some of the country marks on his face. One other negro fellow named ARTHUR, about 3_ years old.. A negro wench named RACHAEL, about 30 years old, very well featured, and not very black; there went with them a negro wench named PHILLIS belonging to Mr. George MAGOUNE; she is wife to the above named JACK. Whoever takes up said negroes and delivers them to me in Salisbury, shall have 40 Shillings reward... Francis LOCK.

(40) Ran away from the Subscriber living near Salisbury, North Carolina, Rowan county, the 16th of October, 1768; a negro fellow named JACK, African born, came from Pennsylvania about two years since... Hugh JENKINS; John MITCHELL; Hugh MC GUNAY (?). October 27, 1769.

(41) Stolen from the subscriber in Granville county..a..pale chesnut sorrel horse.. He is supposed to be stolen by one John JONES, an Irishman.. Said JONES stole the same day, from one Mr. SKINNER, a smooth boar'd gun... Robert HARRIS.

(42) Ran away from the subscriber..October last; a negro fellow named SCOTLAND, about 37 years of age, about 5 ___ 8 inches high.. supposed to be with a negro fellow named PETER, belonging to Samuel SMITH... Jonathan JASPER (?). Novemb. 10th, 1769.

1770 - 1771 - 1772 - No issues located.

1773 - All issues missing except for the following from Harvard University Library-December 24 fragment.

(December 24, 1773.)

(43) A List of Letters remaining in the Post-Office, Newbern.
A. James ANDREW, Orange. B. Thomas BALLARD, William BORBUT, John
BOHANNON, Salisbury (2), John BOYLE, Rowan, Thomas BOURKE, Hills-
borough (2). C. Duncan CAMPBELL, Granville (2), William CHAMBERS,
Orange, George CLARKE, John COLLIER, Neuse, James CRAFORT, Pitt,
William CROIG, Orange, Charles CUPPLES, Bute. D. Nathan. DAVIS,
Carteret, William DAVIS, Pitt, Michael DE BRUEL, William DIXON,
Elisha DOWTY, Beaufort (2), F. Sampson FLEEMING, Joseph FOREMAN,
Hyde, Fulkert FULKERTSON, son of Fulkert DIRICKSON. G. Charles
GALLOWAY, Dan River, James GALLOWAY, Dan River, John GILBERT, Hyde,
John GORDON, Granville, Jacob GREEN, Tryon, H. James HAMILTON,
Currituck, Moses HAMMOND, Orange (2), Robert HARRIS, Granville,
Robert HEATH, Beaufort, John HENDERSON, Mecklenburgh (2), Robert
HENDERSON, Tho. WOLGAN, Orange, Mrs. HOSMER, Onslow, John HOWARD,
Clubfoot's Creek. J. William JAMIESON, Halifax (2), William
JOHNSTON, Orange, Amos JOHNSTON, Carteret, John JONES, Henry IRWIN,
Tarborough. K. Gilbert KERRY, Dobbs, Richard KING, Rowan, William
KUXING, Craven. L. Samuel LEECH, Rowan, Joseph LILLIBRIDGE, Bogue,
Thomas LLOYD, Onslow. M. William MC CLENATKAN, Halifax (3), Lack-
land MC LOUN (?), Charles MC DONALD, Edgecombe, James MC NIETT,
Halifax, John M'___, Carteret (2), John MADDUX, Johnston, Alexander
MARTIN, Guilford, Thomas MERCER, Pitt, William MILLER, Mary MITCHELL,
Joseph MONTFORT, Halifax, John MOROW, Orange, William MOOR, Andrew
MOOR, Hyde, William MUIR, Halifax. N. Sarah NILER. P. James PAIN,
Granville, George PATTEN, Salisbury, William PARK, Pitt. Samuel
PEETE, Northampton (2). Q. Mr. QUANTOCK. (Remainder missing.)

(44) Newbern, December 24. To His Excellency Josiah MARTIN, Esq;
Captain General, Governor, and Commander in Chief, in and over the
Province of North-Carolina. The humble Address of the Council...

1774 - All issues missing except for the following from Harvard
University Library-January 7, December 16, 23. From Department of
Archives and History-July 15-Photostat, September 2-Photostat.
Note-Original of July 15 is found in the New York Public Library.
Original of September 2 is found in the British Public Record Office,
in London, England.

January 7, 1774.

(45) Advertisements. Just imported in the brig Sally, Simon ALDER-
SON, master, from Bristol, by Richard ELLIS, And now opening at his
ready money store in Newbern A Large..assortment of dry Goods...

(46) To be Sold at public vendue, on Thursday the 6th day of January next, Part of the personal estate of George KORNEGE, deceased,
consisting of Hogs, Corn, and sundry Plantation Tools, &c... John
KORNEGE, Jacob KORNEGE, George KORNEGE, Executors.

(47) To be Sold, Five hundred acres of Land in Duplin County; with
a very good House 24 by 24, Brick Chimney, a Kitchen 24 by 16, and
other outhouses..Peach and Apple Trees. Three hundred and seventy
acres adjoining, with a House 24 by 16, with an Orchard of 300 bear-

(47) (Cont.) ing Apple Trees. Two hundred acres, in Duplin..
Also, 900 acres, in Duplin, near the North East of Cape Fear River..
apply to the subscriber, near Duplin Court House. Burwell LANIER.

(48) Run Away, From the Subscriber.. a Negro Man named SHIE, about
Five Feet Six Inches high..talks little or no English..Eight Dollars
Reward... Christopher CHISTIAN. Near Anson Court-House.

(49) For Sale, About 60,000 of White Oak Hogshead Staves, now
ready for Market on Occacock Island. William BURGESS, & Co.

(50) Whereas many of the Persons who have leased Lands belonging
to Richard Dobbs SPAIGHT, a Minor, make a Practice of cutting Fire
Wood for Sale from off the said Lands contrary to the Act of Assembly regarding Orphans Lands, which forbid any Waste to be made on
them; I hereby, on Behalf of the Guardian of said Minor, offer a
Reward of Forty Shillings..(for) any Offender; to be paid on Conviction. Tim. CLEAR. Nov. 19, 1773.

(51) To Be Sold, A Plantation pleasantly situated on the South
Side of Neuse River, about Six Miles below Newbern.. For Terms
apply to Mrs. DEWEY.

(52) Taken up and committed to Goal at Beaufort in Carteret County,
Two new Negroes, they came in a Canoe to Bogue Sound, but where
from we cannot understand. By some Accident, or Act of Humanity,
they got out of Goal, of a cold evening (almost starved even in the
fore part of the Night, and must have inevitably perished before
Morning) and Strayed to the Subscriber's Kitchen, who wishes the
proper Owner had them, but cannot send them any more into Confinement to starve and freeze to Death according to Law: For the Great
Law-Giver Moses, had in Command, that we should do no Murder.
Robert WILLIAMS. Hamlet, Carteret County. Nov. 22, 1773.

(53) To be Sold, The following Tracts of Land, Lots and Houses,
formerly the property of the late Chief Justice HENLEY; to wit, One
Tract containing 400 acres on the south west side of Pee Dee River,
beginning on the south side of Fork Creek, below Tillers fork; 300
acres on the south west side of Pee Dee River, beginning on the
north side of Lynch's Creek; 300 acres on the south west side of
Pee Dee River, beginning on the East side of the north prong of
Fork Creek; 320 acres of Land on the east side of Cape-Fear River,
below Wilmington, near the fork of said River; 500 acres of Land
in Orange County on Mountain Creek, and 113 acres in Chowan County,
near Edenton. Also sundry Lots in the Town of Edenton, and one
House and Lot in the Town of Hallifax. For terms apply to Samuel
JOHNSTON, in Edenton, who is fully impowered by John HENLEY, Esquire,
Heir at Law of the said Chief Justice HENLEY, to make a good title
to the above estates.

(54) Whereas Masters of Vessels, and other Persons make a Practice
of run_____ the Stakes and Beacons fixed in the Channels leading from Newbern to Occacock Bar, to the great Prejudice of the
Navigation, and the manifest Injury of the Subscriber, who is employed by the Commissioners of the Navigation to keep the same up.

(54) (Cont.) I hereby offer a Reward of 40 Shillings for the Discovery of any Person offending..on Conviction. John BRAGGE.

(55) North-Carolina, ss. By his Excellency Josiah MARTIN, Esquire,
Captain General, Governor, and Commander in Chief, in and over the
said province. A Proclamation. Whereas I have received advice from
Major-General HALDIMAND, Commander in Chief of his Majesty's forces
in America, that accounts have been transmitted to him by his Majesty's Superintendent of Indian Affairs in the southern district, of
a most barbarous murder, wantonly, and without provocation, committed by a certain *Hezekiah COLLINS, in the back part of the province
of Georgia, on the bodies of two young Cherokee Indians, which hath
highly exasperated that nation..a reward of 100 Pounds Sterling...
Given under my hand, and the great seal of the said province, at
Newbern, this 18th day of September, 1773, and in the 13th year of
his Majesty's reign. Jo. MARTIN. God save the King. By his Excellency's command, J. PARRATT, D. S. Hezekiah COLLINS is 18 or 19
years of age, 5 feet 5 inches high,..well sett..has dark brown hair,
a very down cast look and of a tawny complexion. *This Proclamation
was some time ago inserted in this Paper, and the Reward offered
for John COLLINS; but by a Deposition..from the Province of Georgia,
the Murder appears to have been committed by Hezekiah COLLINS...

Newbern: Printed by James DAVIS, in Front Street...

(56) Newbern, January 7. In the Assembly, December 18, 1773. The
Bill, for establishing Superior Courts in this Province, was read
the third time, passed, and sent up to the Council... John HARVEY,
Speaker.

(57) To the Freeholders of _____ County. Gentlemen, (Illegible)
Lemuel HATCH, James COOR. Newbern, Jan. 3, 1774.

(58) On Saturday last was married here, Lancelot Crave BERRY, Esq;
Collector of his Port, and only Son of the late Hon. Charles BERRY,
Esq; Chief Justice of this Province, to Miss Sally OUTERBRIDGE, only
Daughter of the late Capt. OUTERBRIDGE, of this Town; a most amiable
young Lady...

July 15, 1774.

(59) Newbern, July 15. By an authentic Account from Cross-Creek,
the Perpetrator of the horrid Murder and Robbery committed there
some time ago..is discovered, and proves to be Mr. Patrick TRAVERS
himself, the Owner of the Store that was robbed, who is now in Gaol
..soon to take his trial for that attrocious Crime.

(60) By Accounts from Philadelphia, as late as the 23d June, we
find there is to be a general Congress there of Deputies from the
several Colonies, on the Twentieth Day of September next, in order
to consult on Ways and Means for the Preservation of America against
the late very extraordinary Acts of Parliament that have been passed,
which we find, by the northern Papers, have spread universal Alarm
there.

(61) Advertisements. Whereas I have received certain Information,
that some People in different Counties of Earl GRANVILLE's District
have presumed to survey vacant Lands..there is not, nor has been
since the Year 1763, any Person empowered to make Surveys of the
vacant Lands in that Part of this Province..every Surveyor will be
prosecuted for so doing. Jo. MARTIN. Newbern, June 10, 1774.

September 2, 1774. Number   .

(Majority of this page is illegible.)

(62) Resolved, That ___ ___ ___ General Congress to be held in
the City of Philadelphia on the 20th of September next, then and
there to deliberate upon the present State of British America, and
to take such Measures as they may deem prudent, to effect the Purpose of describing with Certainty the Rights of Americans, repair-
ing the Breeches made in those Rights, and for guarding them for
the future from any such Violations done under the Sanction of public
Authority. Resolved, That William HOOPER, Joseph HEWES and Richard
CASWELL, Esquires..be Deputies to attend such Congress... Resolved,
That the Moderator of this Meeting, and in case of his Death, that
Samuel JOHNSTON, Esq. be impowered..to convene the several Deputies
of this Province..at such Time and Place as he shall think proper.
Resolved, That the following be Instructions for the Deputies..in
General Congress on the Part of this Colony, to wit. That they
express our sincere Attachment to our most gracious Sovereign King
George the Third, and our determined Resolution to support his lawful Authority in this Province; at the same Time, that we cannot
depart from a steady Adherence to the first Law of Nature, a firm
and resolute Defence of our Persons and Properties, against All
unconstitutional Incroachments whatsoever... John HARVEY, Moderator.

(63) At a very respectable and numerous Meeting of the Freeholders
of the County of Chowan and Town of Edenton, and other Inhabitants
of the said County and Town, at the Court House in Edenton, on the
22d Day of August, in the Year of our L__ 1774, the Rev. Mr. Dani__
EARL in the Chair.. Resolved, ..that the Inhabitants of this Province are entitled to all Liberties, Franchises, and Privileges, of
his Majesty's British Subjects. Resolved, That all Acts of the
British Parliament imposing Taxes or Duties, for the Purpose of
raising a Revenue, to be paid by the Inhabitants of this.. (Colony)
are arbitrary and unjust... Resolved, That the Act for stopping up
the Port of Boston is highly unjust, oppressive... Resolved, That
Samuel JOHNSTON, Thomas OLDHAM, Thomas JONES, Thomas BENBURY, Thomas
HUNTER, and Joseph HEWES, Esquires, be appointed to represent this
County and Town at the Meeting of the Delegates from the several
Counties in this Province at Newbern, the 25th Instant..and to ap-
point Delegates to..a General Congress of Deputies from all the
American Colonies at Philadelphia...

(64) At a Meeting of the Freeholders of the County of Johnston, in
the Province of North-Carolina, at the Court House of said County,
on the 12th Day of August 1774, Samuel SMITH, Jun. Esq; in the
Chair... Resolved, That Samuel SMITH, Sen., Needham BRYAN, Sen.,
William BRYAN, and Benjamin WILLIAMS Esquires, be appointed to appear

12

(64) (Cont.) in our Behalf at such Times and Places as shall be
judged most proper, to meet the Deputies of the other Counties, to
consult the Welfare of America on this alarming Crisis which seems
to threaten our Liberties... Resolved, That Samuel SMITH, sen., William BRYAN, John SMITH, Samuel SMITH, jun., Needham BRYAN, jun.,
Henry RAMS, and William WARD, Esquires, be appointed a Committee to
correspond with the Committees of the other Counties...

(65) At a Meeting of the Freeholders of the County of Anson, in the
Province of North-Carolina, held at the Court House of the said
County on the 15th Day of August, 1774, Thomas WADE, Esq; Chairman...
Resolved, That Samuel SPENCER, and William THOMAS, Esquires be ..
Deputies on Behalf of this County..at the..general Convention of
Deputies from the several Counties, to be held at Johnston Court
House, on the 20th of this instant August... Resolved, That Thomas
DOCKERY, Thomas WADE, Samuel SPENCER, William THOMAS, Charles ROBIN-
SON, Charles MEDLOCK, William PICKETT, and James ___D, be..a Com-
mittee for this County, to correspond with any Committee of Corre-
spondence in this Colony...

(66) At a general Meeting of the Freeholders and Inhabitants of the
Town of Halifax, on Monday the 22d Day of August, 1774, John WEBB,
Esq; being chosen Moderator, the following Resolves were unanimously
agreed to, viz... Resolved, That as Joseph MONTFORT, Esq; our worthy
Representative, from his present Indisposition, cannot possibly attend the General Meeting at Newbern on the 25h..Instant, we hereby
constitute and appoint John GEDDY, Esq;..in his Stead...

(67) At a General Meeting of the Freeholders in the County of Granville, on the 15th Day of August, 1774..we unanimously appoint and
delegate Thomas PERSON and Memucan HALL (?), Esquires to act on our
Behalf at the meeting at Johnston Court House on the 25th Instant..

(68) Philadelphia, In Assembly, July 22. ..Resolved unanimously,
That the Hon. Joseph (?) GALLOWAY, Speaker, Samuel RHOADS, Thomas
MIFFLIN, Charles HUMPHREYS, John MORTON, George ROSS and Edward
BIDDLE, Esquires, be..a committee...

(69) Advertisements. To be Sold at public Vendue. On Thursday the
15th Instant, sundry Household and Kitchen Furniture, Bedding and
Books, Cows and Calves, and one Lot in Newbern..pursuant to the last
Will and Testament of Mary CONWAY, deceased... Edmund WRENFORD, Ex.

(70) Hyde County, Taken up and committed to this County Gaol, by
Order of Barridge Hutchins SILBY, Esq; a Negro Fellow... Seth HOVEY,
Sheriff. August 6, 1774.

(71) Strayed from the Subscriber's Plantation on Brice's Creek..
a..Horse..purchased..of James HARKER at Core-Sound. Whoever will
bring the said Horse to the above..Plantation, or to me at Newbern,
shall receive 30 Shillings reward. Alex. GASTON. August 13, 1774.

(72) Craven County, ss. By James DAVIS and Thomas HASLEN, Esquires,
Two of his Majesty's Justices of the Peace for said County. Whereas
Complaint hath been made to us, by John KENNEDY, that a Negro Fellow

belonging to him, named ABRAHAM, between 20 & 21 Years old, a short
well-made Fellow..ran away from him..June last, and is supposed to
be lurking about, committing many Acts of Felony..by Virtue of an
Act of Assembly..if the said ABRAHAM doth not surrender himself,
and return home..that any Person may kill and destroy the said slave
..without Accusation or Impeachment of any Crime.. Given under our
Hands and Seals, this 12th Day of August, 1774, and in the 14th
Year of our Majesty's Reign. James DAVIS, Thomas HASLEN. N. B.
Whoever brings the said Slave to me alive shall have 40s. and 5s.
for his Head. John KENNEDY.

(73) Newbern, August 4, 1774. The Subscriber..has just opened
School in the public School House of this Town, where he proposes
to teach, at 16 Shillings per Quarter, Reading, Writing, Cyphering,
Navigation and Surveying;-and Algebra, Euclid's Elements, Latin and
Greek, at 18 Shillings... Elias HOELL.

(74) For Sale. An exceeding good Negro House Wench. A very likely
young Negro Fellow... 120 acres of..Land on Beaver Creek, adjoining
the Plantations of Mr. SPEIGHTS (?) and Mr. EDWARDS... Also 500
Acres,..old purchased Land, on the north Side of Neuse River, below
Newbern, on the Heads of Smith's and Piercey's (?) Creeks... For
Terms apply to the Subscriber, at his Plantation on Trent Road, five
Miles above Newbern. Benjamin WHITAKER. August 15, 1774.

(75) Run Away, From the Subscriber, a Negro Fellow, named BUCK,
calls himself Tom BUCK, abou___ ___ feet high, 50 Years of Age, talks
good English... Joseph HANCOCK. Woodstock, August 18, 1774.

December 16, 1774. Number 302.

(76) The celebrated Dr. Benjamin FRANKLIN's Considerations on the
Nature and Extent of the legislative Authority of the British Parliament...

December 23, 1774. Number 303.

(77) Boston, November 3. In Provincial Congress, October 29, 1774.
Ordered, That Captain HEATH, Captain WHITE, Captain GARDINER, Mr.
CHEEVER, and Mr. DEVENS, be a Committee, to wait upon his Excellency
with the following Message. John HANCOCK, President...

(78) North-Carolina, ss. By the Honourable James HASELL, Esq;
President and Commander in Chief in and over the said Province. A
Proclamation. ...I have thought proper further to prorogue the
said Assembly to Tuesday the 24th Day of..January, then to meet at
Newbern... Given under my Hand..at Newbern, this 22d Day of Decem-
ber, 1774. James HASELL... By his Honour_ Com__nd, James PARRATT,
D. S.

1775 - All issues missing except for the following from Harvard University Library-January 13. From New York Historical Society-March
24, April 7, May 5,12, June 30, July 7, 14. From Department of
Archives and History-June 16 - February 24-Photostat-April 14-Fac-
similie-October 6-Photostat-December 22-Photostat. Note: Originals

of February 24 and April 14 found in the British Public Record Office. October 6 and December 22 found in the New York Public Library.

January 13, 1775.

(79) A Certain run away Negro Man, who calls himself GEORGE, came and delivered himself up to the Subscriber on the 19 Ult.; he says he belongs to one Billy THOMAS, in Jamaica..ran away in a Schooner and were 9 Months getting to this Country.. This GEORGE speaks tolerable broken English, may be about 23 _ 24 Years of Age..Notwithstanding the above Pretensions, we judge his Owner must be in South Carolina, altho' the fellow is artful enough to talk about making of sugar, and pretends to be intirely ignorant about any Thing that belongs to the Culture of Rice. Caleb BELL. Beaufort, Carteret County, December 6, 17__.

(80) James VERRIER, Peruke Maker and Hair Dresser, from Boston (?) and Philadelphia, Begs Leave to acquaint the Ladies and Gentlemen in general, that he has taken a Shop in Newbern...

(81) Newbern, January 3, 1775. Just imported in the Ship Harmony Hall, Captain Benjamin GREENAWAY, the following Goods, to be sold by Edward BATCHELOR & Co. for Cash or Country Produce at their Store, Union Point, viz....

(82) Newbern, January 6, 1775, Florence M'CARTHY, Teacher of Mathematics and the English Language, Has opened School in the Academy, where he proposeth diligently to instruct Children...

(83) Newbern, December __, Just imported in the Schooner Hope, Thomas FOSTER, Master, from Africa, a Parcel of likely healthy Slaves Consisting of Men, Women, and Children, are to be sold for Cash, or Country Produce, by Edward BATCHELOR & Co. at their Store at Union Point.

(84) An Order having passed the last County Court, appointing the subscribers Commissioners, and impowering them to build a Draw Bridge over Trent River, at Sw__ing Point..request those who are inclinable __ undertake the Building..to give in their Proposals in __ting... Joseph LEACH, Richard ELLIS, John HAWKS. Newbern, December 29, 1774.

(85) Philadelphia, December 21. In Assembly, Thursday, December 15, 1774. A. M. Upon Motion, Resolved, N. C. D. That the Honourable Edward BIDDLE, Speaker, John DICKENSON, Thomas MIFFLIN, Joseph GALLOWAY, Charles HUMPHREYS, John MORTON, and George ROSS, Esqrs. be, and they are hereby appointed Deputies, on the part of this province, to attend the General Continental Congress, proposed to be held at the city of Philadelphia, on the 10th day of May next; and that they..do meet the said Congress accordingly; unless the grievances of the American colonies shall, before that time, be redressed... Ordered, That Mr. THOMPSON, Mr. BROWN, Mr. CHAPMAN, Mr. PEARSON, Mr. John JACOBS, Mr. WAYNE, ____ EWING, Mr. ALLEN, and Mr. EDMONDS, __ committee to prepare and bring in draughts __nstructions for the Deputies to the ensuing Con_ress, and of a circular letter to the Speakers of the several colony Assemblies, informing them of the proceed-

(85) (Cont.) ings of this House on the report of their Delegates at
the late Congress... Extract from the Journals, Charles MOORE,
Clerk of Assembly.

(86) Newbern, January 13 (?). Last Friday Night died, universally
and deservedly lamented, in the 18th Year of her Age, Miss Dorothy
RICHARDSON... Her Remains ____ by a considerable Number of res____ -
able Persons, were, on Monday Evening, interr__ in Christ Church
Burying Ground.

(87) Advertisements. Craven County, ss. By Thomas HASLEN, and
James DAVIS, Esquires, Two of his Majesty's Justices of the Peace
for said County. Whereas Complaint hath been made to us, by Frederich FONVEILLE, that a Negro Fellow named JEM, about 23 Years old,
..and a Negro Wench named GRACE, of a yellowish Complexion, and
about 25 Years old, bothe belonging to him, ran away from him, a_d
are supposed to be lurking about, committing many Acts of Felony..
if the said JEM and GRACE doth not surrender themselves, and return
home..any Person may kill and destroy the said Slaves..without Accusation or Impeachment of any Crime...10th Day of January 1775...
Thomas HASLEN, James DAVIS.

(88) Newbern, February 24. On Sunday last was married, at Pen___,
Seat of Abner NASH, Esq; near this Town, Robert (?) MOORE, of Cape
Fear, to Miss ____ NASH, daughter of the late Thomas NASH ____ of
Edenton, a most amiable young Lady, with a handsome Fortune.

(89) Chowan County, January 28. (Majority of this article is illegible;) ...We do..heartily and sincerely declare and profess ____
are sorry for our Misconduct,... William ROBI____, John HILL (?),
Demsey BOND.

(90) Chowan County, Jan____ __. The Committee of this County ___
_ ___ House of Mr. John C____ and _ chosen Mr. Luke SUMNER their
Chairman _ Mr. Samuel JONES their Clerk. Resolves, 1. That the
Thanks of this Committee ____ ____ to Joseph HEWES, Esq; for the
faithful D____ of his Duty as a Delegate from this Province..at the
Continental Congress. 2. That a Subscription be promoted in this
County, under the direction of Mr. Luke SUMNER, Capt. James SUMNER,
____ Col. Edward VAIL... Manufacturies, viz. Wire, Wool and Cotton
Cards, Fulled Woollen Cloth, Bleached Linen, and Steel. Signed by
Order of the Chairman. Samuel JONES, Clerk.

(91) At a Meeting of the Committee for the Town of Edenton, on Sat-
urday the 4th of February, 1775. Present Robert HARDY, Joseph HEWES,
Robert SMITH, Jasper CHARLTON, John ROMBOUGH, William BENNETT,
Charles BONDFIELD, Thomas JONAS, John GREEN. Robert HARDY, Esq;
Chairman. The Chairman acquainted the Committee, that Mr. William
LITTLEJOHN, Merchant, had informed him, that sundry Goods, lately
imported in the Ship Peggy, William PATTON, Master, from Leith, in
Great Britain..had just arrived in Edenton consigned to him, which
he was willing to deliver up to the Committee, to be by them disposed
of agreeable to the tenth Article of the American Continental Asso-
ciation. ..Mr. Archibald CAMPBELL..had also imported in the said
Ship Peggy a Box of Linens..which he was willing to deliver up to the

(91) (Cont.) Committee... Resolved, That all the said Goods be sold at public Vendue..for ready money; and that Robert HARDY, Joseph HEWES and Robert SMITH, see this Resolve carried into Execution... By Order of the Committee, Charles BONDFIELD, Clerk.

(92) Perquimans County, February 11, 1775. The respective Counties and Towns in this Colony are requested to elect Delegates to represent them in Convention who are desired to meet at the Town of Newbern on Monday the 3d Day of April next. John HARVEY, Moderator.

(93) Ran away from the Plantation of John MURRAY, Esq; at Rocky Point..a Negro Wench named HANNAH, formerly the Property of Patrick GORDON, Esq; late of this Town... 5 Pounds reward. Newbern, February 23, 1775.

(94) North-Carolina, ss. By his Excellency Josiah MARTIN, Esquire, ..Governor..in and over the said Province. A Proclamation. Whereas a most daring Robbery was committed on Friday the 3d of February Instant, by two Men, supposed to be from the Province of Virginia, in the House of Mr. John FOY, Planter, near Newbern.. John FOY..has offered a Reward of One Hundred Pounds, Proclamation Money; I have thought proper, for the more speedy bringing to Justice these desperate Offenders, to issue this Proclamation..to..require and command, all Magistrates and other Officers...(illegible)... Jo. MARTIN, By his Excellency's Command, James PARRATT, D. Sec.

(95) If Mr. Joseph WRIGHT, Son of Mr. Michael WRIGHT, of the City of Bristol (?) be living, he is requested to apply to the Printer hereof, who will inform him of a considerable Legacy left him by his Uncle Mr. Joseph NOTT (?), of the Island of Jamaica. Mr. WRIGHT left Bristol some Years ago and went to Virginia, where 'tis supposed he lived with a Company of Merchants...

March 24, 1775. Number 316.

(96) Philadelphia, February 1. Proceedings of the Convention for the Province of Pennsylvania, held at the State-House in Philadelphia, January 23, 1775, and continued by Adjournments to the 28th. The Chairman of the Philadelphia Committee opened the Convention by explaining the Motives which induced said Committee to propose the holding this Convention. Joseph REED, Esq; was chosen President of this Convention. Messrs. Jonathan B. SMITH, John BENEZET, and Francis JOHNSON, Esq; were chosen Secretaries.

(97) North-Carolina, ss. By his Excellency Josiah MARTIN, Esquire, His Majesty's Captain General, Governor, and Commander in Chief, in and over the said Province, &c., &c., &c. as special Commissioner, Agent and Attorney, for the Conduct and Management of the Estate, Affairs and Concerns, of the Right Honourable Robert Earl GRANVILLE, William CLAYTON, Esquire, and Lady Louisa CLAYTON, his Wife. ..In Virtue of which Power of Attorney, I Do hereby claim, demand and take Possession of all and singular the Lands, Messuages...belonging to the said Earl GRANVILLE, William CLAYTON and Lady Louisa CLAYTON, his Wife, within this Province... 7th Day of March, Anno. Dom. 1775. Jo. MARTIN.

(98) Beaufort County, ss. By Moses HARE and John PATTEN, Esquires, Two of his Majesty's Justices of the Peace for said County. Whereas Complaint hath been made to us by John ROBINSON, that a Negro Slave belonging to him, named JACK, about 25 Years of Age, about 5 Feet 7 Inches high, a black Country born Fellow;..and is supposed to be lurking about, doing Acts of Felony in this Province. ..And we do.. command the Sheriff of the..County of Beaufort, to make diligent Search after the above mentioned Slave..if the said JACK doth not surrender himself, and return home..that any Person..may kill and destroy the said Slave..without Impeachment or Accusation of any Crime... 9th Day of March, 1775... Moses HARE, John PATTEN.

(99) Beaufort County, ss. By Thomas PEARCE and Christopher RESPESS, Esqrs., Two of his Majesty's Justices of the Peace for said County. Whereas Complaint hath been made to us by Thomas BONNER and Isaac PATRIDGE, that a Negro Man Slave belonging to the Estate of John MAULE, Esq; deceased, hired by them for one Year, ending in October next, (named ADAM) about 5 Feet 10 Inches high, a Country born Fellow, about 38 Years of Age, ran away from them..and is supposed to be lurking about, committing many Acts of Felony..the Sheriff of the..County of Beaufort, to make diligent Search..if the said ADAM doth not surrender himself, and return home..any Person may kill and destroy the said Slave..without Accusation... 9th Day of March, 1775... Thomas PEARCE, Christopher RESPESS. N. B. The above named ADAM was hired by us to the Complaints, and will warrant the above Proclamation or Advertisement. Moses HARE, John PATTEN, Reading BLOUNT, Jun. Executors.

(100) The noted Horse Bajazett Stands at Ellis's Square in Newbern ... Richard ELLIS. Newbern, March 3, 1775.

(101) The Subscriber's Horse Telemachus Will stand the ensuing Season at Pembroke, four Miles above Newbern, on Trent River... A. NASH. March 14, 1775.

(102) The Subscriber intending for the West Indies about the End of this Month, begs the Favour of those who are indebted to him..speedily to settle... Bartholomew ROOKE. Newbern, March 10, 1775.

April 7, 1775. Number 318.

(103) Newbern, April 7. The General Assembly being prorogued to the 27th of March..(then) from Day to Day to the 4th Instant... Colonel John HARVEY, their late Speaker, was then unanimously elected, and conducted to the Chair accordingly. The House then waited on his Excellency..who..opened the Session with the following Speech... Jo. MARTIN.

(104) North-Carolina, Chowan County, March 4, 1775. The Committee met at the House of Capt. James SUMNER, and the Gentlemen appointed at a former Meeting Directors to promote Subscriptions for the Encouragement of Manufactures, informed the Committee that the Sum of 80l. Sterling was subscribed by the Inhabitants of this County for that laudable Purpose. ... Signed by Order of the Committee. Samuel JONES, Clerk.

(105) Advertisements. Bute County, March 26, 1775. Run away from the Subscriber, on Thursday Evening last, a Slave of the Indian Blood, named CHARLES, of a very light Complexion... William TABB.

(106) Came to my Plantation eight Miles from Newbern..a white Horse ... M. HOWARD. March 24, 1775.

(107) To all to whom these Presents may come. Know Ye, that whereas I Mary M'GEHE, Wife of Joseph M'GEHE, of the County of Bute, in the Province of North-Carolina, being dissatisfied with my said Husband, and having eloped from his Bed for upwards of eight Months past in which Time I have been gotten with Child by another Man..and being fully determined not to live with him more during my Life, nor at any Time hereafter to cohabit with him the said Joseph M'GEHE, and, in Consideration of..one Hundred and Twenty Pounds Value in Effects, Part of his Estate, which I hereby acknowledge to have received.. and in Consequence..I do hereby Covenant and agree..that I never will..depend on him as my Husband..but from this Day forward look on myself as divorced from him... And the said Joseph, on his Part, doth..agree..that we the said Joseph and Mary, have this Day most solemnly agreed before God and the World, to be no longer Man and Wife..this 29th Day of August, 1769. Joseph M'GEHE, Mary M'GEHE. Signed and acknowledged in the Presence of Robert GOODLOE, Thomas JACKSON.

Earl of Dartmouth's Mss. April 14, 1775. Number 319.

(108) Newbern, April 14. North-Carolina, ss. At a General Meeting of Delegates of the Inhabitants of this Province, in Convention at Newbern, the 3d Day of April, in the Year 1775. For Anson County, ___. Beaufort, Roger ORMOND, Thomas RESPISS, Jun. Bladen, Green HILL, James RANSOM, Thomas EATON. Brunswick, John ROWAN, Robert HOWE. Bertie, John CAMPBELL, David STANDLEY, John JOHNSTON. Craven, James COOR, Lemuel HATCH, Jacob BLOUNT, William BRYAN, Richard COG-DELL, Joseph LEECH. Carteret, William THOMPSON, Solomon SHEPHERD. Currituck, Thomas MACKNIGHT, Francis WILLIAMSON, Samuel JARVIS, Solomon PERKINS, Nathan POYNER. Chowan, Samuel JOHNSTON, Thomas OLDHAM, Thomas JONES, Thomas BENBURY, Thomas HUNTER. Cumberland, Thomas RUTHERFURD, Farquard CAMPBELL. Chatham, ___. Dobbs, Richard CAS-WELL, William MC KINNE, Simon BRIGHT, Junior, George MILLER. Duplin, Thomas GRAY, Thomas HICKS. Edgecomb, ___. Granville, Thomas PERSON, John PENN, Robert MONTFORT, Robert WILLIAMS, Memucan HUNT. Guilford, Alexander MARTIN. Hyde, ___. Hertford, George WYNNS, Joseph WORTH, Halifax, Willie JONES, Benjamin M'CULLOCH, Nicholas LONG. Johnston, ___. Mecklenburg, ___. Martin, ___. New Hanover, William HOOP-ER, John ASHE. Northampton, Allen JONES, Jeptha ATHERTON. Orange, Thomas HART, Thomas BURKE, John KINCHEN, Francis NASH. Onslow, Edward STARKEY, Henry RHODES, William CRAY. Perquimons, John HARVEY, Benjamin HARVEY, Andrew KNOX, Thomas HARVEY, John WHEDBEE, Jun. Pasquotank, Jonathan HEARRING, Edward EVERIGIN, Isaac GREGORY, Joseph JONES, Joseph READING. Pitt, John SIMPSON, Edward SALTER, James GORHAM, James LANIER, William ROBSON. Rowan, Griffith RUTHERFORD, William SHARP, William KENNAN. Surry, ___. Tryon, ___. Tyrrell, Joseph SPRUIL, Benjamin SPRUIL, Jeremiah FRAZER. Wake, John HINTON, Michael ROGERS, Tignal JONES. Newbern, Abner NASH, James DAVIS.

(108) (Cont.) Edenton, Joseph HEWES. Wilmington, Cornelius HARNETT.
Bath Town, William BROWN, Halifax Town, John WEBB, Joseph MONTFORT.
Hillsborough, ____. Salisbury, ____. Brunswick Town, Parker QUINCE.
Campbelton, Robert ROWAN. ...The Delegates then proceeded to make
Choice of a Moderator, when Col. John HARVEY was unanimously chosen,
and Mr. Andrew KNOX appointed Clerk. ...The Association entered
into by the general Congress at Philadelphia, on the 20th Day of
October, in the Year of our Lord 1774, ...was presented to this Convention by Col. Richard CASWELL; and..was read. Resolved, That this
Convention do highly approve of the said Association, and do for
themselves agree to adhere to the said Association... In full Approbation and Testimony whereof, the Members of this Convention subscribed their names..except Mr. Thomas MACKNIGHT, who refused. Resolved, That the Conduct of William HOOPER, Joseph HEWES, and Richard CASWELL, Esquires, in the Meeting..at Philadelphia was in every
particular worthy of the sacred Trust reposed in them... On Motion,
Resolved, That William HOOPER, Joseph HEWES, and Richard CASWELL,
Esquires, be, and..are hereby appointed Delegates, to attend the
General Congress to be held at Philadelphia on the 10th Day of May
next... Mr. Thomas MACKNIGHT, a Delegate for the County of Currituck, having been called upon to sign..the Association approved of
by the Continental Congress held at Philadelphia, thereupon refused,
and withdrew himself. Resolved, That in the Opinion of this Convention, that from the disingenuous and equivocal Behaviour of the said
Thomas MACKNIGHT, it is manifest his Intentions are inimical to the
Cause of American Liberty, and we do hold him up as a proper Object
of Contempt to this Continent and recommend that every Person break
off all Connection, and have no future commercial Intercourse or
Dealing with him... Attested by John HARVEY, Moderator. Andrew
KNOX, Clerk.

(109) The Continental Association was not signed by the Members in
this Convention, as might be presumed from the Publication of their
Clerk. We, the Subscribers, Samuel JARVIS, Solomon PERKINS, and
Nathan POYNER, late Representatives for the County of Currituck, in
a Convention of Deputies for the Province of North-Carolina, held at
Newbern on the third Day of April, 1775, and Jonathan HEARRING and
Isaac GREGORY,..for the County of Pasquotank,_having found ourselves
under the disagreeable Necessity of withdrawing from the said Meeting, and being denied the Justice of having our Reasons entered on
the Journals of their Proceedings (that is, by an express Refusal to
the Representatives for Currituck, which was the only Cause that
those for Pasquotank did not apply) have only this Resource left for
vindicating our Conduct to the World, and rescuing the Character of
a Gentleman we greatly esteem from undeserved Obloquy and Reproach.
The facts..are simply these: Upon its being moved and seconded..
that a Vote should pass, expressing a high Approbation of the Continental Association, Mr. Thomas MACKNIGHT, a Representative for Currituck..got up and declared that he was greatly concerned that he
could not heartily concur in the Vote proposed to be past, on Account
of particular Circumstances in his Situation which obliged him to
dislike some part of the Association; that he owed a Debt in Britain,
which the Operation of the Non-Exportation Agreement would disable
him to pay... Samuel JARVIS, Solomon PERKINS, Nathan POYNER, Isaac
GREGORY, Jona. HEARRING.

(110) Advertisements. This is to give..Notice, that there is a Negro Fellow named HOLLOW, detained from me, he is about 30 Years of Age, a short well set Fellow...five Pounds reward... Benjamin BLOUNT March 10, 1775.

(111) Twenty Shillings Reward. Strayed from the Subscriber living near Dawson's Creek..a dark bay Mare... Tho. W. PEARSON. Craven County, April 13, 1775.

May 5, 1775. Number 322.

(112) Newbern, May 5. By a Vessel arrived here on Wednesday last from Rhode-Island..: Newport, April 22. By a Gentleman from Cambridge we are informed, that between 11 and 12 o'Clock on Tuesday Evening last, a Detachment, consisting of the Grenadiers and light Infantry, amounting to 1000 or 1500 Men, as is reported, embarked from Boston in the long Boats belonging to the Ships of War, and passed Charles River from the western Part of Boston, landed in Cambridge and immediately proceeded towards Concord through Minotamy and Lixington, at which Place last mentioned,..arrived before Sun set, and found 100 Provincials under Arms-The commanding Officer of the advanced Guards addressed them in the most abusive Terms, calling them damned Rebels, &c. demanded of them what Business they had there; and upon being answered they were exercising, commanded them to disperse, threatening to fire upon them if they refused. The Captain of the Provincials not immediately complying, the advanced Guard made two Fires upon them, killed two or three, and wounded six, who died the same Day of their Wounds, upon which they dispersed.

The Regulars marched on to Concord.. By this Time a Number of Provincials had collected, upon which the Detachment began to retreat Exasperated to the highest Degree by the dastardly, merciless Massacre of their Brethren at Lixington, they pursued, and fired upon the Regulars in their Retreat. Earl PERCY, at the Head of a Reinforcement of 1000 Men, with two Field-Pieces, met the Detachment at Lixington, and supported their Retreat. The Provincials still collecting, took to the Fields, and from thence to the Side of the Hills, galled the Regulars severely on their Retreat, and did not quit the Pursuit till they reached Charlestown, when the Regulars encamped upon what is called Bunkers Hill, in the Afternoon of the same Day.. The next Day the Troops took Boats and landed in Boston...

(113) At an Inferior Court of Pleas and Quarter Sessions held for the County of Pitt, April Term, 1775. Present, John HARDY, George MOY, Dempsey GRIMES, William ROBINSON, William BRYANT, Benjamin BOWERS, Edmund WILLIAMS, John WILLIAMS, and John TYSON. A New Commission of the Peace was produced and read in Court, whereby it appeared that several of the most respectable Gentlemen in the County aforesaid, who were in the former Commission, were designedly omitted for which Reason every Gentleman nominated in the new Commission aforesaid, then in Court, except John TYSON, expressly refused to qualify to the same, being all of Opinion that such Qualification would be a Dastardly Condescention which would for ever have disgraced them...

(114) Hyde County, April 25, 1775. At his Seat, in this County,
died, on the 20th Inst. Samuel SMITH, Esq; who for his moral and
social Virtues was universally and deservedly lamented. His Remains
were..on Friday..interred, as being a Colonel, with military Honours.

(115) New-York, April 13. Yesterday Afternoon arrived John SULLI-
VAN and John LANGDON, Esqrs. Delegates for the Province of New-Hampshire, on their Way to the Grand Continental Congress, to be held
at Philadelphia the 10th of next Month.

(116) The following Letter came by the Earl of Dunmore, Capt. LAW-
RENCE, just arrived from London. London, January 30, 1775. "From
unquestionable Authority I learn, that about a Fortnight ago, Dispatches were sent from hence by a Sloop of War to General GAGE, containing, among other Things, a Royal Proclamation, declaring the
Inhabitants of Massachusetts-Bay and some others in the different
Colonies, actual Rebels; with a blank Commission to try and execute
such of them as he can get hold of;-with this is sent a List of Names
to be inserted in the Commission as he may judge expedient. I do
not know them all, but Messrs. Samuel ADAMS, John ADAMS, Robert
Treat PAYNE, and John HANCOCK, of Massachusetts-Bay; John DICKENSON,
of Philadelphia; Peyton RANDOLPH, of Virginia; and Henry MIDDLETON,
of South-Carolina; are particularly named, with many others.-This
black List, the General will, no Doubt, keep to himself, and unfold
it gradually, as he finds it convenient..."

(117) Advertisements. Craven County, ss. By John HAWKS, and
Lancelot Grave BERRY, Esquires, Two of his Majesty's Justices of the
Peace for said County. Whereas Complaint hath been made to us, by
James BIGGLESTON, That a Negro Slave belonging to him, named JEM,
about 28 Years of Age, a stout likely Fellow, about 5 Feet 7 Inches
high; and is Country born..hath run away from his said Master, and
is supposed to be lurking about doing Acts of Felony in this Province...if the said JEM doth not surrender himself, and return home
...any Person..may kill and destroy said Slave..without Impeachment
or Accusation...3d Day of May, 1775... John HAWKS, L. G. BERRY.
N. B. The above Negro Slave is supposed to be harboured or kept out
by his Wife, named RACHEL, a Wench belonging to Mr. Isaac FONVIELLE
.. Reward of three Pounds... James BIGGLESTON.

(118) All Persons indebted to the Estate of Capt. John RICHARDSON,
deceased, are requested to make Payment, to enable me to finish my
Administration next County Court... Tho. HASLEN, Adm. May 4, 1775.

(119) Runaways. Eloped from the Subscribers on Wednesday the 26th
Inst. two newly imported Men Slaves, named KAUCHEE and BOOHUM, about
6 Feet high, and, perhaps, 30 Years of Age. They absconded..about
two Months ago, and were taken up at Broad-Creek, about 10 Miles off,
and brought back by William GATLING of that Place... Forty Shillings
reward from Edward BATCHELOR & Co. Newbern, April 27, 1775.

(120) Eloped from the Brigantine Friendship, in July, 1774, two in-
dented Servants, viz. George TAVERNOR, about 18 Years old, very slender, and pitted with the small-Pox, and calls himself a Groom or
Horse Jockey. Edward GILKS, about 23 Years old, a short hump'd Back

(120) (Cont.) Person with Red Hair, and is by Trade a Curryer or Leather Dresser. 'Tis supposed said Servants are working at or near Newbern. Also ran away in August last, a new Negro Fellow, by Name QUAMINO, about 4 Feet 10 Inches high, and about 30 Years of Age.,his Teeth are filed, and is marked with his Country Marks; had on when he went away, a Collar about his Neck with two Prongs, marked G. P., and an Iron on each Leg. Whoever delivers said white Servants and Negro to Henry YOUNG in Wilmington shall receive 6 1. Proc. Money for the Whole, or 40s. for each... Wilmington, April 10, 1775.

(121) Taken up on Adam's Creek, and committed to the Public Gaol in Newbern, on Saturday the 8th of this Instant, a short well set Negro Man, near five Feet high, about 30 Years of Age, full faced, Country Marks in his Temples, and his Teeth filed sharp, (supposed to be the same Slave some Time past committed to Carteret County Gaol)... Joseph CRISPIN, P. G. Newbern, April 20, 1775.

May 12, 1775. Number 323.

(122) Williamsburg, April 29. The ship Trident, from York river, we hear, is employed by Government for the detestable purpose of transporting troops to Boston. Captain James MITCHELL (being a true friend to his country) has refused to be continued commander of the vessel on that account.

(123) Notice. The Situation of our Affairs, and the Resolves of the Continental Congress, for preventing all Exportation after the first Day of September next, obliges us to call on our good Friends, who are in Arrear to us, either by open Account, Bond, or Note, to make immediate Payment, in order that we may be enabled to make our Remittance to Britain (where we are justly indebted) before the Non-Exportation Agreement takes place, as we are desirous strictly to adhere to that as well as all other the Resolves of that Grand Convention... The Administrators of James DALZELL, deceased, Mess. John BURNSIDE, & Co. and Doctor Joseph DOUSE, have left their Books, Bonds, and Notes of Hands, in our Possession, with proper Authority to receive their Debts, those who are in Arrear to these Gentlemen, will be as expeditious as possible in paying off their respective Ballances. David BARRON, & Co. Newbern, May 10, 1775.

(124) Newbern, May 6. The following Account is just received by Express, in 12 Days from Wallingford, in Connecticut. Wallingford, Monday Morning, April 24, 1775. Dear Sir, ...The King's Troops being reinforced a second Time, and joined as I suppose, .;by the Party who were intercepted by Col. GARDNER, were then encamped on Winter Hill, and were surrounded by 20,000 of our Men, who were intrenching. Col. GARDNER's Ambush proved fatal to Lord PIERCEY, and another General Officer who were killed on the Spot the first Fire. To counterballance this good News, the Story is, that our first Man in Command (who he was I know not) is also killed. It seems they have lost many Men on both Sides. Col. WADSWORTH had the Account in a letter from Hartford..you must immediately send a Couple of stout, able Horses, who may overtake us at Hartford possibly, when we must return Mr. NOY's, and M'COY's, if he holds out so far.. I am in the greatest Haste, Your entire Friend and humble Servant, James LOCKWOOD. N. B.

(124) (Cont.) Col. GARDNER took 9 Prisoners, and 22 clubbed their Firelocks, and came over to our Party... Isaac BEARS.

(125) Philadelphia, April 24, 1775. An express arrived..this evening: Watertown, Wednesday Morning, near 10 o'Clock, To all Friends of American Liberty. Be it Known, that this Morning, before Break of Day, a Brigade, consisting of about 1000 or 1200 Men, landed at PHIPPS Farm, at Cambridge, and marched to Lexington, where they found a Company of our Colony Militia in Arms, upon whom they fired, without any Provocation, and killed six men, and wounded four others ... The Bearer, Trial BRISSET, is charged to alarm the Country, quite to Connecticut, and all Persons are desired to furnish him with fresh Horses... 'Pray let the Delegates from this Colony see this; they know Col. FOSTER, one of the Delegates. J. PALMER, One of the Committee. A true Copy from the Original, by Order of the Committee of Correspondence, of Worcester. April 1775. Attested and forwarded by the Committees of Brookline, Norwich, New London, Lyme, Saybrook, Killingsworth, E. Guilford, Guilford, Brandford, Newhaven. Fairfield, Saturday, April 22, 8 o'Clock. Since the above written..the following by a second Express, Thursday, 3 o'Clock Afternoon...from Woodstock..the Contest between the first Brigade that marched to Concord was still continuing this Morning at the Town of Lexington, to which said Brigade had retreated.. N. B. The Regulars, when in Concord, burnt the Court-House.. I am, &c. E. B. WILLIAMS. To Col. O. B. JOHNSON, Canterbury. P. S. Mr. M'FARLANE of Plainfield, Merchant, has just returned from Boston, by way of Providence, who conversed with an Express from Lexington.. informs that 4000 of our Troops had surrounded the first Brigade.. who were on a Hill in Lexington..there were about 50 of our Men Killed, and 150 of the Regulars. The above is a true Copy, as received by Express from Newhaven, and attested by the Committee of Correspondence from Town to Town. Attest. Jonathan STURGIS, Andrew ROWLAND, Thaddeus BURR, Job BANTRAM, Committee. The above was received Yesterday at 4 o'Clock by the Committee of New-York, and forwarded to Philadelphia by Isaac LOW, Chairman of the Committee at New-York.

(126) Dobbs County, ss. By Henry GOODMAN, and Robert WHITE, Esquires, Two of his Majesty's Justices of the Peace for said County. Whereas Complaint hath been made this Day to us, by John COURT, that a Negro Man named CHARLES, about 20 Years old, Country born, a short, thick, well set Fellow, and of a black Complexion, hath absented himself from his said Master, and is supposed to be lurking about, committing many Acts of Felony in this Province..if the said CHARLES doth not surrender himself, and return home..any Person..may kill or destroy the said Slave..without Accusation.. 29th Day of April, 1775... Henry GOODMAN, Robert WHITE.

June 16, 1775. Number 328,

(127) Affidavits and Depositions, Relating to the Commencement of the late Hostilities in the Province of Massachusetts Bay..Charles THOMSON, Secretary. We Solomon BROWN, Jonathan LORING, and Elijah SANDERSON, all of lawful age, and of Lexington, in the county of Middlesex, and colony of the Massachusetts-Bay, in New-England, do testify and declare, that on the evening of the 18th of April,

(127) (Cont.) instant, being on the road between Concord and Lexington, all..on horses, we were about 10 of the clock suddenly surprized by nine persons, whom we took to be regular officers, who rode up to us, mounted and armed, each having a pistol in his hand,..swore if we stirred another step, we should be all dead men, upon which we surrendered ourselves. They detained us until two o'clock the next morning in which time they searched and ____ having first enquired about the magazine at Concord, whether any guard were posted there, and whether the bridges were up, and said four or five regiments of regulars would be in possession of the ____ town. They then brought us back to Lexington, cut the horses bridles and girt__,turned them loose, and then left us. Solomon BROWN, Jonathan LORING, Elijah SANDERSON. Lexington, April 25, 1775.

(128) Lexington, April 25, 1775. Simon WINSHIP, of Lexington, in the county of Middlesex..being of lawful age, testifieth and saith, that on the 19th of April instant, about four o'clock in the morning ..passing the public road in said Lexington..unarmed, about two miles and an half distant from the meeting-house in..Lexington,..was met by a body of the King's regular troops, was commanded to dismount.. and ordered to march in the midst of the Body..till he came within about half a quarter of a mile of said meeting-house where an officer commanded the troops to halt..prime and load..the said troops marched till they came within a few rods of Capt. PARKER's company, who were partly collected on the place of parade, when said WINSHIP observed an officer at the head of said troops, flourishing his sword, and with a loud voice giving the word fire, fire..instantly followed by a discharge of arms from said regular troops..WINSHIP is positive ..that there was no discharge of Arms on either side till the word fire was given by said officer... Simon WINSHIP.

(129) Lexington, April 25, 1775. I John PARKER, of lawful age, and Captain of the Militia in Lexington, do testify and declare, that on the 19th instant..was informed that a number of regular troops were on their march from Boston..to take the province stores at Concord, ordered our Militia to meet on the Common in said Lexington, to consult what to do, and concluded not to be discovered, not meddle or make with said troops..unless they should insult or molest us; and upon their sudden approach I immediately ordered our Militia to disperse and not to fire.-said troops made their appearance and rushed furiously, fired upon and killed eight of our party, without..provocation therefor from us. John PARKER.

(130) Lexington, April 24th, 1775. I John ROBINS..do testify..that on the 19th inst. the company under the command of Capt. John PARKER being drawn up..on the green or common, and I being in the front rank there suddenly appeared a number of the King's troops..at..about 60 or 70 yards from us, huzzaing and on a quick pace towards us — being wounded, I fell, and several of our men were shot dead by me. Capt. PARKER's men I believe had not then fired a gun...John ROBINS.

(131) We, Benjamin TIDD, of Lexington, and Joseph ABBOT, of Lincoln, in the county of Middlesex..of lawful age, do testify..that on the morning of the 19th of April instant about five o'clock, being on Lexington Common, and mounted on horses, we saw a body of regular

25

(131) (Cont.) troops marching up to the Lexington company, which
was then dispersing; Soon after the regulars, fired, first a few
guns..pistols, ..and then the full (?) regulars fired a volley or
two, before any guns were fired by the Lexington company... Benjamin TIDD, Joseph ABBOT.

(132) (Many of the names in the next deposition are illegible.)
Lexington, April 2_, 1775. We, Nathaniel ____, Philip RUSEL, Moses
HARRINGTON, jun., ____ and David (?) HARRINGTON, William ____,
William TIDD, _____, James WYMAN, Thaddeus HARRINGTON, John
CHANDLER, Joshua REED, jun., Joseph SIMONDS (?), Phineas SMITH, John
C____R, jun., Reuben LOCK, Joel VILES (?), Nathan REED, Samuel TIDD,
Benjamin LOCK, Thomas WINSHIP, ____, ____, Joshua REED, Ebenezer
PARKER, John (?) HARRINGTON, Enoch WALLINGTON, John____, ____ ,
____ STEARNS, ____..inhabitants of Lexington.... Whilst our backs
were turned on the troops we were fired upon by them, and a number
of our men were instantly killed and wounded. Not a gun was fired
by any person in our company..before they fired on us... Signed by
each of the above Deponents.

(133) Lexington, April 25, 1775. We, Nathaniel PARKHURST, Jonas
PARKER, John MUNROE, jun., John WINSHIP, Solomon PIERCE, John MOZEY
(?), Abner MEEDS, John BRIDGE, jun., Ebenezer BOWMAN, William MUNROE
the 3d, Micah HAGER, Samuel SAUNDERSON, Samuel HASTINGS, and James
BROWN, of Lexington,..all of lawful age..we were faced towards the
regulars then marching up to us,..began to disperse when the regulars fired on the company before a gun was fired by any of our Company on them... Signed by each of the above Deponents.

(134) Lexington, 25th of April, 1775. I Timothy SMITH, of Lexington..being of lawful age.. I saw a large body of regular troops
marching up towards the Lexington company then dispersing, and..saw
the regular troops fire,..before the latter fired a gun... Timothy
SMITH.

(135) Lexington, April 25th, 1775. We Levi MEAD, and Levi HARRING-
TON, both of Lexington..and of lawful age..being on Lexington Common, as spectators, we saw a large body of regular troops marching
up towards the Lexington company, and some..on horses..we took to be
officers, fired a pistol or two..on the Lexington company, which was
then dispersing: These were the first guns..fired..immediately followed by several vollies from the regulars... Levi HARRINGTON, Levi
MEAD.

(136) Newbern, June 16. By a Gentleman from Salisbury, we have an
Account, that the famous Joseph POTTAWAY had been tried at the Court
of Oyer and Terminer lately held there, for a Robbery, had been con-
victed, received Sentence of Death, and was to be executed. This is
the Person who in Company with Jacob ODAM, robbed Mr. John FOY, as
mentioned in this Paper some time ago. ODAM surrendered himself to
Government, and is now in this Gaol. ... The Father of ODAM accompanied his Son here, and on Suspicion of his being accessary to the
many Felonies committed by him, has been committed to Gaol...

(137) Charlotte Town, Mecklenburg County, May 31. This Day the Com-

(137) (Cont.) mittee do appoint Colonel Thomas POLK, and Doctor Joseph KENNEDY, to purchase 300 lb. of Powder, 600 lb. of Lead, and 1000 Flints; and deposit the same in some safe Place, hereafter to be appointed by the committee. Signed by Order of the Committee, Eph. BREVARD, Clerk of the Committee.

(138) Williamsburg, May 13. Fredericksburg, Committee Chamber, Saturday the 29th of April, 1775. At a Council of one hundred and two members, Delegates of the Provincial Convention, officers and special deputies of 14 companies of light horse, consisting of upwards of 600 well armed and disciplined men..now rendezvoused here in consequence of an alarm occasioned by the powder being removed from the country magazine in the city of Williamsburg..the 21st instant, and deposited on board an armed schooner by order of his Excellency the Governor. The Council having before them the several matters..particularly a letter from the Hon. Peyton RANDOLPH, Esq; Speaker of the late House of Burgesses of Virginia...

(139) At a Committee appointed and held for Hanover County, at the Courthouse, on Tuesday the 9th of May, 1775. Present, John SYME, Samuel OVERTON, William CRAGHEAD, Meriwether SHELTON, Richard MORRIS, Benjamin ANDERSON, John PENDLETON, John ROBINSON, Nelson BARKELEY (?) and George DABNEY, junior. Agreeable to a Resolution of the Committee held at Newcastle the 2d Instant,..they being full informed of the violent Hostilities committed by the King's Troops in America, and of the Danger arising to the Colony by the Loss of the Public Powder, and of the Conduct of the Governor..and therefore recommending Reprisals to be made upon the King's property..it appears that the Volunteers who marched from Newcastle, to obtain Satisfaction for the Public Powder..proceeded..as follows, to wit, "That an Officer with 16 Men was detached to seize the King's Receiver General, with Orders to detain him.. The said Receiver General not being apprehended, owing to his Absence from home, the..Detachment..proceeded to join the main Body on its March to Williamsburg; and the Junction happened the 3d Instant, at DONCASTLE's Ordinary.. A little after Sunrise the next Morning, the commanding Officer being assured that proper Satisfaction, in Money, should be instantly made, the Volunteers halted..and the following Receipt was given, to wit, "DONCASTLE's Ordinary, New Kent, May 4, 1775, received from the Hon. Richard CORBIN, Esq; his Majesty's Receiver General, 330 l. as a Compensation for the Gun powder lately taken out of the Public Magazine by the Governor's Order..." Test, Patrick HENRY, Jun. Test, Samuel MERIDITH. Parke GOODALL.

It was then considered, as that a General Congress would meet in a few Days..the commanding Officer wrote the following Letter, and sent it by Express. Sir, May 4, 1775... Your most humble Servant, Patrick HENRY, Jun. To Robert Carter NICHOLAS, Esq; Treasurer. Test, Samuel MEREDITH, Garland ANDERSON... Ordered, That the Clerk do transmit a Copy of these Proceedings to the Printers... By order of the Committee, Bartlett ANDERSON, Clk.

(140) Norfolk, May 25. By a Gentleman..we are informed, that the Hon. Peyton RANDOLPH, Esq; was elected President of the Grand Congress, and Charles THOMPSON, Esq; Secretary; that the Hon. Benjamin

(140) (Cont.) FRANKLIN, Esq; Agent for several Provinces, had
lately arrived from England, and was unanimously appointed by the
General Assembly of Pennsylvania one of the Delegates for that Province, as was also the Hon. Thomas WILLING, Esq;-that Joseph GALLO-
WAY, Esq; had not thought proper to make his Appearance in the Congress.

(141) Advertisements. To be sold at the Court-House in Newbern,..
several very likely high Blooded Mares with Foals by their Sides,
got by the Subscriber's Horse Telemachus. Abner NASH. June 14,
1775.

(142) In Obedience to the Commands of his Excellency the Governor..
I hereby warn all the Freeholders in the County of Craven and Town
of Newbern, to meet at the Court House in Newbern on Friday the 23d
of this Month, and elect for the Town of Newbern one, and for the
County of Craven two, proper Persons to represent the said Freeholders in the ensuing Assembly. John BRYAN, Sheriff. June 9, 1775.

(143) Ran away from the Subscriber on the 25th Day of July, 1774.
Five new Negro Men-CATO..about 6 Feet high, and about 25 Years old..
CUDJOE, about 6 Feet high..with his Country Marks down his cheeks..
about 20 Years of Age. JUNE, about 30 Years of Age and about 5 Feet
10 Inches high. SEPTEMBER, about 25 Years of Age..about 5 Feet 6
Inches high.. MAYSON, about 25 years of Age, about 5 Feet 3 Inches
high... They are all of the Guinea Country.. Whoever..delivers any
of them..at my Plantation near Purrysburgh (?); shall receive a Reward of 12 Dollars each, if in South Carolina, and if in any other
Province, 24 Dollars each... John STROBHAR (?).

June 30, 1775. Number 330.

(144) Newbern, June 30. On Friday last, the Election for Members
of Assembly for this Town, and County of Craven, was held at the
Court-House, when Abner NASH, Esq; for the Town, and Mr. James COOR,
and Col. William BRYAN, for the County, were unanimously elected.
Lemuel HATCH, Esq; one of our late worthy Members for this County,
having declined.

(145) Advertisements. North-Carolina. By his Excellency Josiah
MARTIN, Esq; Captain General, Governor.. A Proclamation. Whereas
I have received certain Information that sundry ill disposed Persons
have been..going about the County of Brunswick, and other Counties
of this Province, industriously propagating false, seditious, and
scandalous Reports, derogatory to the Honour and Justice of the King
and his Government.... Given under my Hand..at Fort Johnston, 16th
Day of June, 1775. Jo. MARTIN.. By his Excellency's Command.
Alexander MACLEAN, pro James BIGGLESTON, D. S.

(146) For Sale. A Valuable Negro Man seasoned to the Country. J.
W. STANLY. June 28, 1775.

(147) Agreeable to the last Will and Testament of Mrs. Elizabeth
FULMORE, deceased, at her late Dwelling House in Newbern..the 13th
Day of July next, will be sold at Public Vendue, the said Dwelling

(147) (Cont.) House, with the Lot of Land..household Goods and Effects... James COOR, Executor. Newbern, June 16, 1775.

July 7, 1775. Number 331.-

(148) In Congress. Monday, June 12, 1775.. This Congress..considering the present critical, alarming and calamitous State of these Colonies, do earnestly recommend, that Thursday, the Twentieth Day of July next, be observed by the Inhabitants of all the English Colonies on this Continent, as a Day of public Humiliation, Fasting, and Prayer... By Order of the Congress, John HANCOCK, President. (A true Copy.) Charles THOMSON, Secretary.

(149) Wilmington, June 26. At a general Meeting of the several Committees of the District of Wilmington, held at the Court-House in Wilmington, Tuesday the 20th of June, 1775. Whereas his Excellency Josiah MARTIN, Esq; hath, by Proclamation..and read this Day in the Committee, endeavoured to persuade, seduce and intimidate, the good People of this Province from taking Measures to preserve those Rights and that Liberty, to which, as Subjects of a British King, they have the most undoubted Claim... We, the Committees of the Counties of New-Hanover, Brunswick, Bladen, Duplin, and Onslow, Do unanimously resolve, that, in our Opinion, his Excellency Josiah MARTIN, Esq; hath, by the said Proclamation..discovered himself to be an Enemy to the Happiness of this Colony in particular, and to the Freedom, Rights and Privileges, of America in general... Richard QUINCE, Sen. Chairman.

(150) Newbern, July 7. Committee Chamber, Beaufort County, June 23, 1775. Alderson ELLISON, being conscious that he had made many illegal and unwarrantable Expressions against the General Congress and this Committee came into the Committee, and made the following Concessions, which was received, and approved of by them.. I Alderson ELLISON, of the County of Beaufort, having said many illegal..things against the General Congress, and the Committee of said County, tending to mislead the Inhabitants thereof..Do sincerely ask Forgiveness of all my Countrymen..for the future I will use every Means..to preserve and defend the Rights and Liberties of my Country. Alderson ELLISON.

(151) June 22, 1775. By Letters from the Congress of the 19th of June..Col. WASHINGTON, of Virginia, is appointed General and Commander in Chief of all the American Forces; General WARD, of the Massachusetts, and General LEE, to be Major Generals; Major GATES, of Virginia, to be Adjutant General, with the Rank of Brigadier.. Col. Philip SCHUYLER to be second in Command of the New-York Forces.

(152) On Friday last, agreeable to his Excellency's Writ of Election the Freeholders of the County of Pitt attended at the Town of Martinsborough, and elected Col. John SIMPSON, and Mr. Edward SALTER, their old Representatives...

(153) The Sloop Temperance, Paul WHITE, Master, lying at Indian Land, in Pitt County, was dismasted and set on Fire by the Lightning on Tuesday last.

July 14, 1775. Number 332.

(154) South-Carolina. In Provincial Congress, Charlestown, Wednes-
day, June 21, 1775. Ordered That the Hon. William Henry DRAYTON,
the Hon. Capt. Barnard ELLIOT, Col. Charles PINCKNEY, Col. James
PARSONS, Col. Isaac MOTTE, Col. Stephen BULL, Col. William MOULTRIE,
Major Owen ROBERTS, Capt. Thomas SAVAGE, Capt. John HUGER, Miles
BREWTON, Thomas FERGUSON, and Gabriel CAPERS, Esquires, be a Deputa-
tion to present to his Excellency the Governor the Address of this
Congress. South Carolina. To his Excellency the Right Honourable
Lord William CAMPBELL, Governor, and Commander in Chief in and over
the Province aforesaid,... Published by the Order of the Congress,
Peter TIMOTHY, Secretary.

(155) Cambridge, June 15. (The following infamous Proclamation has
been handed about here, and is now re-printed to satisfy the Curios-
ity of the Public.) By his Excellency the Hon. Thomas GAGE, Governor and Commander in Chief in and over his Majesty's Province of
Massachusetts Bay, and Vice-Admiral of the same. A Proclamation.
... The Minds of Men having been thus gradually prepared for the
worst of Extremities, a Number of armed Persons, to the Amount of
many Thousands, assembled on the 19th of April last, and from behind
Walls and lurking Holes attacked a Detachment of the King's Troops,
who..made Use of their Arms only in their own Defence. .. I do
hereby, in his Majesty's Name, offer and promise his most gracious
Pardon to, all Persons who shall forthwith lay down their Arms, and
return to the Duties of peaceable Subjects, excepting only from the
Benefit of such Pardon Samuel ADAMS and John HANCOCK, whose Offences
are, of too flatitious a Nature to admit of any other Consideration
than that of condign Punishment. ... I do hereby publish, proclaim,
and order, the Use and Exercise of the Law Martial, within and
throughout this Province..whereof all Persons are hereby required to
..govern themselves as well to maintain Order..among the peaceable
Inhabitants..as to resist, or encounter and Subdue, the Rebels and
Traitors above described... Given at Boston, this 12th Day of June
..1775. Thomas GAGE. By his Excellency's Command, Tho. FLUCKER,
Sec'ry.

(156) New-York, June 26. The Ship Juliana, Capt. MONTGOMERY, arrived at Sandy-Hook last Saturday Night from London..our worthy
Governor came Passenger. He landed..Yesterday Evening, and was conducted to the House of the Hon. Hugh WALLACE, Esq; by an immense
Number of the principal People of this City.

(157) The following Account came to Hand, by Post from Watertown,
about 10 Miles from Boston, taken from a Paper printed at that place,
by Mr. Benjamin EDES, formerly a Printer in Boston. Watertown, June
19. Friday Night last a Number of the Provincials intrenched on
Bunker-Hill in Charlestown; and on Saturday about Noon a large Number
of Regulars from Boston came across Charles's River, and landed a
little below the Battery near the Point, where bloody Battle commen-
ced. The very heavy Fire from the Shipping obliged the Provincials
to retreat a little this Side Charlestown Neck about Sunset, when
the Enemy took Possession of our Entrenchment; after which they set
the Town of Charlestown on Fire, beginning with the Meeting-House,

(157) (Cont.) and we hear they have not left one Building unconsumed.

(158) Copy of a Letter sent to the Committee of this City. Gentlemen,..I am an American, of Newbury Port, New-England: On my arrival here the 19th instant from the Mediterranean, I was informed of the care you had taken with regard to the exportation of bread and flour to this island, especially in the instance of Capt. TAVERNER, commander of a ship belonging to Isaac and Benjamin LESTER, of Pool, in England, and loaded by T. BEACH, of New-York; which LESTERS are notedly enemies to American Liberty, as appears by the petition of the town of Pool, for an exclusive right to the fishery on the banks of Newfoundland... Messrs. Robert and Benjamin JENKINS have at all times declared their fixed determinations to do nothing to the prejudice of the American Cause. Mr. Robert BULLEY is also our stedfast friend.,: Jonathan PARSONS, Jun. St. John's, Newfoundland, May 30, 1775. To the Committee of Safety for the city of New-York. P. S. If you judge the above representation deserves your attention..beg the favour of your writing a letter,..to the Hon. Benjamin GREENLEAF, Esq; at Newbury Port, New England, to be communicated to the Committee of Safety for that place, whose joint testimony will doubtless set my character in its true light... J. PARSONS, Jun.

(159) Philadelphia, June 28, By an Express,.we have the following Account of the Battle at Charlestown on Saturday the 17th of June Instant... This Account was taken from Capt. Elijah HIDE, of Lebanon, who was a Spectator on Winter's Hill during the whole Action.

(160) Major Thomas MIFFLIN is appointed Aid de Camp to General WASHINGTON...

(161) Yesterday an Express..from the Camp near Boston..Col. B. LINCOLN, Hingham, Monday. Yesterday I came out of Boston..I heard the Officers and Soldiers say, that they were sure that they had a thousand or more Men killed and wounded..General HOWE commanded the Troops; they buried their Dead at Charlestown, among whom was Major PITCAIRN... Job BRADFORD. Copy. June 20, 1775. The Dead and Missing on our Part are about 60 or 70. The above Account of Captain BRADFORD's is confirmed by two other Channels, and agree.

(162) Newbern, July 14. Dobbs County, Committee Chamber, July 5, 1775. Mr. George MILLER informed the Committee that divers injurious and scandalous Reports have, and still do prevail in this and neighboring Counties, tending to represent him as a Person inimical to American Liberty... Resolved, That the aforesaid Charge is altogether unjust, ungenerous, and without Foundation... Resolved, That Mr. James DAVIS be requested to publish the aforesaid Resolve in the Newbern Gazette. By Order, J. GLASGOW, Chairman.

(163) We hear from Salisbury, that this Province is at last delivered from that Pest of Society Joseph PETTAWAY, one of the Persons that robbed Mr. FOY, and who has committed, with one Jacob ODAM, a Man now in this Gaol, and others; the most daring Robberies..in America. This Man made his Exit at the Gallows in Salisbury, on the 30th of June last, pursuant to his Sentence, for a Robbery committed at the

(163) (Cont.) House of Mr. BELL of Guilford County...

(164) Advertisements. By his Excellency Josiah MARTIN, Esquire..
A Proclamation... By his Excellency's Command, John COLLET, pro
James BIGGLESTON, D. Sec.

(165) Craven County, By Joseph LEECH and Thomas HASLEN, Two of his
Majesty's Justices of the Peace for said County. Whereas Complaint
hath been made to us by Henry VIPON, that a Negro Slave, named BILLY,
a yellow Fellow, he formerly belonged to the Estate of the Rev. Alex.
STEWART, and is well known about Durham's Creek..ran away from him,
and is supposed to be lurking about, committing many Acts of Felony
..if the said BILLY doth not surrender himself, and return home..any
Person may kill and destroy the said Slave..without Accusation or
Impeachment of any Crime... 12th Day of July, 1775. Joseph LEECH.
Thomas HASLEN. N. B. Whoever brings the Head of the said Slave to
me, shall have Five Pounds Reward. Henry VIPON.

October 6, 1775. Number 344.

(166) Philadelphia, August 16. Extract of a letter from Frederick
Town, August 1. ..I have had the happiness of seeing Capt. Michael
CRESSAP, marching at the head of a formidable company, of upwards of
130 men from the mountains, and back woods, painted like Indians,
armed with tomahawks and rifles, dressed in hunting shirts and mock-
asons, and..some of them had travelled near 800 miles from the banks
of the Ohio...

(167) Advertisements. North Carolina, New Hanover County. Soon
after a Meeting of the Inhabitants of the County,..it was..agreed,
that the Delegates..should be instructed, in Case the Provincial
Congress should..judge it necessary to raise Troops for the Defence
of this Province..Col. John ASHE be appointed to the first Command...
We were induced to give these instructions from a long Knowledge of
upwards of 25 Years of that Gentleman's meritoriousServices in his
military Capacity, as well as in his other Public Offices; but as
the said Congress..have appointed Officers..under whose Command we
choose not to risque our Lives and Properties... Resolved, That we
will not act, either as Officers or Soldiers, under the Command of
any of the Officers of the present Appointment, either on the Pay
of the established Troops, Minute or Militia, and will immediately
form ourselves into independent Companies of Rangers, under Officers
of our own choosing...

(168) Whereas a Report was raised and spread about, the 12th or
15th November past, in the Neighbourhood of Peacock's Bridge, Dobbs
County, that a certain John BANKS was there most inhumanly murdered
..much to the Prejudice of the Characters of innocent Persons..as
will appear from the following Deposition of..John BANKS... That he
John BANKS,..near the 15th of November past borrowed a Horse of Jesse
ACCOCK (?)..to ride to Peacock's Bridge, at which Place Mr. Zachariah MASON had advertised the Public he would take a Boat out of his
Pocket in which a Man should cross Contentny Creek..he sat in to
drinking..that Day out, the ensuing Night, and the next Day until
about two o'Clock P. M. that then he went up Stairs (at COOPER's,

32

(168) (Cont.) the Person who then lived at the Bridge) and went to
sleep..he received no Wound... John BANKS. Sworn to before us this
__th Sept. 1775. James DAVIS, Tho. HASLEN.

(169) Craven County, ss. By Robert ORME and Thomas WEBBER, Esquires
two of his Majesty's Justices for said County. Whereas Complaint
hath been made to us by Joseph BROCK, that a Negro Man named BILLICO,
about 21 Years of Age, about 5 Feet 9 Inches high, a black well set
Fellow, Country born, well known in this County, formerly the property of Josiah HOLT, is supposed to be lurking about, and committing
many Acts of Felony..if the said Slave-doth not surrender himself,
and return home..then any Person may kill or destroy the said Slave..
without Accusation or Impeachment of any Crime... 28th of August,
1775. Robert ORME. Thomas WEBBER.

(170) Newbern, August 9,.1775. The Subscriber requests all Persons
who are any Way indebted to him to make Payment as speedy as possible
to enable him to satisfy his Creditors-The noted..Tavern in which he
lives to be let, and the Furniture, &c. to be sold cheap..and will
let the Plantation..within four Miles of this Town, between Neuse
and Trent Roads... Edmund WRENFORD.

(171) To be Let, by the Subscriber, for the Term of 10 Years, on
moderate Rent, Several Thousand Acres of..Lands..on the South Side
of Trent River... A. NASH.

December 22, 1775.

(172) Newbern, December 22. In Committee of Safety for the District
of Edenton. Nov. 21, 1775. From a number of depositions that were
read in this Committee, which gave..reason to think that the conduct
of Cullen POLLOK, Esq; was inimical to the common cause of America..
that Gentleman voluntarily offered to subscribe the test directed
by the late Provincial Congress, and..he was discharged..and in order
to prevent any injury to his Character, do order this to be made
public. By order of the Committee. Charles BONDFIELD, Secretary.

(173) In Committee of Safety for the District of Edenton, Dec. 1,
1775. Whereas certain persons, notwithstanding the examination
which Cullen POLLOK, Esquire, underwent before this Committee, and
..had acquitted him, did on the night of the 21st day of November
last..in the most violent, lawless, and riotous manner, break into
the house of the said Cullen POLLOK, take him out of his bed, force
him through the streets, and treat him with..brutality disgracefully
shocking to humanity. This Committee, in order to express their ab-
horrence of such infamous proceedings, do..declare the promoters and
abettors of that horrid transaction, to be worthy of public contempt
... Charles BONDFIELD, Secretary.

(174) Advertisements. On Wednesday the 3d of January will be sold
at public vendue, at the dwelling-house of the deceased Mr. Timothy
CLEAR, in Newbern. The Household Furniture..Rum..Molasses..Sugar,
cotton and wool Cards..on the succeeding day..all the Stock... David
BARRON, John HAWKS, James COOR, Administrators. Newbern, Dec. 19,
1775. Also will be sold..same time and place, about 25 likely Slaves

(174) (Cont.) they being my dividend of the slaves belonging to the estate of Mr. CLEAR... Archibald CAMPBELL.

(175) Run away from the subscriber..a man slave, of the Indian breed..whoever delivers him to me in Bute County shall have 10 pounds ... William TABB.

(176) I John TYSON; from the fullest conviction, solemnly and sincerely declare that I have been pursuing mean ___ ___ of the liberties of America in general, and ___ ___ ___ of this colony, and truly conscious of the heinousness of my guilt ___ now publicly confess the same, and solemnly..promise that I will for the future support and defend...the constitutional rights and liberties of America ... John TISON.

(177) Beaufort County, Dec. 2, 1775. Whereas I have been suspected as a person inimical to the liberties of America, I take this method to acquit myself... Isaac PATRIDGE.

(178) Georgia, November 1, 1775. To all men..Patrick MACKAY Esq; of the island of Sa___ in the province of Georgia hereby gives notice of a most daring and ___ robbery and piracy and requests their aid and assistance to seize, stop, and bring to punishment the perpetrators of the crime... About 11 o'clock on the night of Tuesday the 31st of October, 1775, nine armed men came on board a schooner, then lying moored off the point of Sapello..in Georgia, cut both her cables..and proceeded immediately to sea. Of the perpetrators of this piracy two only are yet known-Samuel PRICE and Samuel WELLS. PRICE is a short slim man, rather well made, about 35 years of age.. WELLS is a tall slender young man, about 25 years of age, and was born in Rhode Island. There were on board the schooner..a white man John BACON, and three negro men.. A reward of 50 Dollars.. And likewise a reasonable and generous Salvage for recovering and delivering the said schooner to Mr. Alexander ROSE, merchant, in Charlestown, South Carolina, or to me, in Georgia... Patrick MACKAY.

(179) ___ Petersburg, October 28, 1775. The business lately under the management of Mr. Archibald CUNISON, deceased, on account of Mess. BUCHANANS, HASTIE, and Co., merchants in Glasgow, we have put into the hands of Mr. Robert MC KITTRICK, who will ___ ___ Halifax town, for the purpose of settling..the debts due to their Milner's store in Virginia, and their Halifax, Deep Creek, Windsor, and Orange stores in North Carolina... William BUCHANAN, Andrew MC KINZIE, Attornies for BUCHANANS, HASTIE, and Co.

(180) North Carolina, Edgcomb County, Nov. 20, 1775. The subscriber gave a bond of 42 (Remainder illegible.) Edmund (?) MARSH.

(181) On the first day of January ___ will be sold..Several Tracts of Land..cattle, sheep and horses..hired out, for one year, several Negroes.. The land and Negroes being part of the estate of Major Joseph MOORE, deceased,... The Executors. Tarborough, Nov. 13, 1775.

(182) Craven (?) County, ss. By Joseph LEECH and James DAVIS, Esquires, two of his Majesty's Justices for said County. Whereas Com-

(182) (Cont.) plaint hath been made to us by Thomas J. EMERY, that a Negro Man named BOB, about 6 Feet high..is supposed to be lurking about, committing many Acts of Felony..if the said Slave doth not surrender himself, and return home..any Person may kill or destroy said Slave.. 17th of November, 1775. Joseph LEECH. James DAVIS. N. B. Whoever apprehends and secures the said Slave..shall have 40s. if brought alive, or 5 1. for his Head. Thomas James EMERY.

1776-No issues located.

1777 - Filmed from the originals in the University of North Carolina Library - The following issues missing-January through June; December 19.

July 4, 1777. Number 3_3.

(183) Fish-Kill, May 29. ... June 5. Capt. David HAWLEY, of Stratford, has taken ___ vessels in the sound, one loaded with provisions going ___ w-York; 14 Tories were taken on board, among who_ ___ a certain Capt. RICE of New Haven, now in goal in tha_ ___ n...

(184) Advertisements. State of North Carolina, Craven County, ss. By Richard ELLIS and Alexander GASTON, Esqrs. two of the Justices for the said County. Whereas Complaint hath been made to us by Richard BLACKLEDGE, that a Negro Man named DUBLIN, about 30 Years of Age, is a New-Negro, and speaks broken English, he is about five feet six Inches High, of a Yellowish Colour, and has sharp filed Teeth, also a Negro Lad named BURR, about 16 Years old, is Black..belonging to the Estate of Timothy CLEAR, deceased, which were hired by said BLACKLEDGE, of the Administrators of said Estate..the 12th Day of February 1777, for one Year, both of which Negroes immediately ran away... (Torn) ___ver apprehends the said Negroes, and carries ___ Salt Works, at Core Sound..shall have for each of them four Dollars ... Richard BLACKLEDGE.

(185) Proposals For printing by Subscription. An exact Abridgement of all the Acts of Assembly of this State in Force and Use, alphabetically digested.. ___ He begs Leave, as he is now solliciting the Favour of the Public on another Publication, to return them his most sincere Thanks for their great Encouragement to..his Revisal of the Laws, and Office of a Justice.. As he is now detached from the Service of the Public as Printer to the State, in which honourable Service he has laboured Twenty Eight Years, he is quite at Leisure, and..will publish the Book with..Expedition. James DAVIS.

(186) Wilmington, June 23, 1777. Run away from the Subscriber in Wilmington..a Negro Slave named BEN, about 22 Years of Age, 5 Feet 6 or 8 Inches high.. The above Negro was purchased by the Subscriber in December last of Col. William TAYLOR, who had him of Col. Edmund TAYLOR, in Mecklenburg County, Virginia, and he had him of Col. John WILLIAMS, in Granville County,.. Ten Dollars Reward, if taken in this State... William WILKINSON.

(187) To be Sold by the Subscriber, (Torn) ___asant and valuable Plantation he lives on..Corn &c. now growing. Also a fine Stock of

35

(187) (Cont.) _____ Horses, Plantation Tools,..House-___ ___itchen Furniture, a few good Blankets, Sheets, and ___e Linen, China Ware, Quart Bottles, some Wool;..Books, ___w, History, &c. also three or four valuable Negroes, &c. M. HOWARD. June 25, 1777.

(188) Newbern, June 27, 1777. Run away from Green Spring near Newbern, a Negro Fellow named SMART, very black, about 5 Feet 8 Inches high.. He is supposed to be lurking about Slocomb's Creek, with a Fellow belonging to Mr. ALMOND, and a Gang of Runaways belonging to the late Mr. CLEAR's Estate... Five Dollars Reward. James DAVIS.

(189) The Subscriber has for Sale, at his Store in Newbern, two Dozen Pair of Philadelphia made Cards, which will answer for Cotton and Wool. Richard COGDELL. June 20, 1777.

(190) Newbern, June 27, 1777. A few Tickets in the States Lottery to be sold by Richard ELLIS.

(191) June 13, 1777. Deserted from the second North Carolina Continental Battalion, in the Month of December 1775, John BECK, a young Man about 22 Years of Age, 5 Feet 10 Inches high, of a light Complexion, light Hair, blue Eyes, and well made. He was inlisted in Hertford County, but it is expected he will be harboured in Edgcomb or Dobb's County, near Peacock's Bridge.. Reward of Twenty Dollars... Hardy MURFREE, Maj. 2d Battalion.

(192) Wilmington, June 5, 1777. The Copartnership of HARNETT and WILKINSON being near expiring, they propose selling the Lot of Ground in Wilmington whereon the Stillhouse now stands..Warehouse..three Stills, with Worms and Tubs..largest..will hold near 2000 Gallons.. Cisterns, Pumps... William WILKINSON.

July 11, 1777. Number 384.

(193) Philadelphia, June 12. Extract of a letter from Providence dated June 2. "This day I saw Mr. ____, who informs me of his mother, Mrs. ____, coming from Newport by a flag last Saturday week; she says ..she was at the house of Mr. John MILLER, who came in and said 'the jig is over with us.' Mrs. MILLER asked why.. He answered..that a French war was inevitable. Good news to hear of the tories crying out 'the jig is over.'"

(194) Extract of a letter from Sinepuxent, dated June 4. "On Sunday the 1st instant the schooner Hawke, Zephaniah ELDRIDGE, bound from Boston to Alexandria ran ashore near this place."

July 18, 1777. Number 385.

(195) Charlestown, (S.C.) June 5. On Saturday the Brigantine of war Comet, Capt. ALLEN, returned from a cruize, in which he took one prize .. Captain OGILVIE, who was master of the Apalachicola..and was a passenger in her when taken by Capt. ALLEN, informs us, that in the end of December last..to the westward of Bermuda, he fell in with the sloop Mary, Thomas JONES master, from Edenton to Cape Nichola Mole, then a mere wreck. Captain OGILVIE took the master and his six sail-

(195) (Cont.) ors on board, and carried them to England. In the
Downs the sailors were pressed by a boat from the Speedwell sloop of
war; some of them giving information that Capt. JONES had been lieutenant of an American privateer, he was also taken away, and was on
the Speedwell...

(196) On Friday last arrived at a safe port the sloop Polly, late
Capt. HENDERSON, from Missisippi... bound for Dublin; taken off the
Havannah on the 13th instant, by the privateer sloop Vixen, Captain
Downham NEWTON, of this port.

(197) Yesterday arrived at a safe port the prize sloop Adriadne,
William FREEMAN, late master, from the Musquito shore, bound for Jamaica..taken on the 3d inst..by the Washington privateer of this port,
commanded by Capt. ANTHONY.

(198) Advertisements. The Subscribers for the Virginia Gazette of
Mess. DIXON & HUNTER, and Mr. Alexander PURDIE,..are hereby requested
to pay up the Balance for the Years expired.. And in order that the
Subscribers whose Year is not yet expired may not be at a Loss, I have
taken the Liberty to insert their Names, and the Time on which their
last Payment will become due, viz. William GOOD 20th July, James GREEN
17th August, John BARRY 24th August, Isaac GUION 21st September, David
FORBS 21st September; so far DIXON & HUNTER. Alexander PURDIE, viz.
Robert SHAW, Esq; 5th July, Captain John DALY, William RANDALL, and
Philip CHEYNEY, the 9th August, Edward WHITTY 16th August; Abner NASH
Esq; 23d August, Major John BRYAN, George CLARK, and James LITTLE,
30th August; William BLOUNT and John CORT, 14th September, Dugald
CAMPBELL and Shadrich FULSHER, 20th September, John CARRUTHERS and
Edmund HATCH, 26th September, Joseph MARSHALL, Jarvis BUXTON, and
Joseph ASHBURY, 11th October, Jesse COBB 8th November next. Richard
COGDELL.

(199) Newbern, July 17, 1777. Wanted, a Quantity of clean Flaxseed..
by Edward BATCHELOR and Company.

(200) Newbern, July 17, 1777. For Bourdeaux, in Old France, The Ship
Harmony Hall, William PILE Master, has excellent Accomodations for
Passengers: For Passage apply to Edward BATCHELOR and Company, or
said Master on Board at their Wharf.

(201) July 17, 1777. Run away from the Subscriber..a Negro Man
named DICK, about 5 Feet 8 Inches high.. Whoever delivers the said
Negro to me on Great Contentney in Dobbs County, shall have Three
Pounds Reward, or Forty Shillings if delivered to Mr. David THOMSON
in Newbern. Everitt HOUSE.

July 25, 1777. Number 386.

(202) Philadelphia, July 2. Extract of a letter from Gen. WASHING-
TON to Congress, dated camp at Quibble town, June 25, 1777. Sir,
When I had the honour to address you last, it was on the subject of
the enemy's retreat from Brunswick to Amboy, and of the measures pur-
sued to annoy them... G. WASHINGTON. Published by order of Congress.
Charles THOMSON, Secretary.

(203) Newbern, July 25. Since our last, a large Vessel from this
port has sailed, having on Board a great Number of Tories, with their
Wives and Families.. Among them is Mr. Martin HOWARD, late Chief
Justice of this Province, with his Wife and Daughter.

(204) Advertisements. Newbern, July 24, 1777. Ten Dollars Reward.
Deserted from my Company in the 5th North-Carolina Battalion of Con-
tinental Troops, sundry Soldiers, viz. William WATSON, William TOP-
PING, and John ROBINSON, new Recruits; also Nathan GRAY, Willie GUR-
GANUS, William SATHERTHWAITE, Elijah SLADE, Thomas WILKINSON, John
KENNEDY, Andrew HUSTON, Christopher SHERMAN, William MOORE, George
WEST, Benjamin ALEXANDER, Henry and Anthony TULLY, John and William
GE_REL, and Simon FITZGERALD, all belonging to this State... Benja-
min STEDMAN, Capt. 5th Regiment.

(205) Newbern, July 25, 1777. Three Dollars Reward. Run away from
the Subscriber, a Negro Man named SURRY, about 5 Feet 6 Inches high,
about 30 Years of Age, well made, is rather yellowish.. He was formerly the Property of Governor TRYON, and now belongs to the Estate
of Isaac EDWARDS, deceased... Richard BLACKLEDGE, Jun.

August 1, 1777. Number 387.

(206) Philadelphia, In Congress, June 16, 1777. Ordered, that the
Letters which have passed between Gen. WASHINGTON and Gen. HOWE, on
the Subject of Exchange of Prisoners, be published, and that the several Printers of Newspapers thoughout the Continent be requested to
insert them. Charles THOMSON, Secretary.

(207) Advertisements. Newbern, July 24, 1777. Whereas it has been
reported in this Town that the Subscriber did (in York-Town, Virginia)
act inimical to the Cause of American Freedom, and left said town in
a precipitate and clandestine Manner; he therefore calls upon any
person or persons, who can prove the same, to do so in the most public
Manner, as his character is injured by said report. John LOWRY.

(208) Craven, August 1, 1777. Run Away From the Subscriber in May
last, a dark Mulatto Man Slave called BEN,..about 50 Years of Age..
well known on Pamplico River, as he formerly belonged to one Mr. WAR-
WICK, of that Place... William BRYAN.

(209) Craven, August 1, 1777. Run away From the Subscriber, living
on Clubfoot's Creek..a Negro Slave named SAM, formerly the Property
of Henry CHEW, deceased, a stout well made Fellow, of a yellowish
Complection..near six Feet high.. He is a Cooper by Trade, and may
attempt to get to Virginia or Maryland, as he has sisters and Brothers
there..if taken in this State..20 Dollars, and if out thereof 30 Dollars. Lovick JONES.

(210) Craven, August 1, 1777. Run Away From the Subscriber, living
at the Head of Clubfoot's Creek,..a Mulatto Slave named BEN, about
5 Feet 8 Inches high..20 Dollars if taken in this State, and 30 Dollars if out thereof... Richard LOVETT.

August 8, 1777. Number 388.

(211) Advertisements. Newbern, August 4, 1777. Wanted immediately for the celebrated..Brig of War, Sturdy Beggar, under Command of James CAMPBELL, Esq; now fitting out at this Place for a short Cruize against the Enemies of the Thirteen United States, a few good Seamen and Marines.. For the Encouragement of such Seamen as may choose to enter on Board said Vessel, Twenty Dollars Bounty will be given...

(212) Newbern, July 31, 1777. Whereas the Subscriber intends to the West Indies in the Course of a few Weeks, any Person having Demands on him are desired to apply for immediate Payment... Wilson BLOUNT.

August 15, 1777. Number 389.

(213) Extract from the Minutes. Published by order of Congress. Charles THOMSON, Secretary. June 23, 1777. Resolved, That Joseph TRUMBULL, Esq; commissary general..be directed to supply the army with provisions..until the commissaries general on the new establishment shall be prepared to enter upon the business.

(214) Newbern, August 15. Advertisements. To be Sold at public Vendue, on Friday the 5th of September, at the late dwelling house of George Pheney LOVICK, dec. All the personal Estate of said Deceased.. Horses, Hogs, Cattle, Sheep, Household Furniture... Anne LOVICK, Wm. M. HERRITAGE, Admrs. August 12, 1777.

August 22, 1777. Number 390.

(215) Newbern, August 22. Arrived here since our last, the Sloop Viper, Captain STOW, from Martinique, in 20 Days; and at Wilmington, the Brig Adventure, Hugh SCATER Master, from Hispaniola.

August 29, 1777. Number 391.

(216) Boston, July 10. Whereas many persons have believed it to be impossible to bore cannon that have been cast solid, this matter is past doubt..there is..in the common, two pieces carrying 12 pound ball, one of brass, the other of iron, which were both cast solid at Titticut, and were bored solid, by the new machine established at Bridgewater, upon the model and proportions given by Louis MARESQUELLE, Colonel in the artillery, and chief founder of brass and iron cannon in this state.

(217) Charles-Town, (S.C.) July 7. Two armed brigs belonging to this port, commanded by Charles and Francis MORGAN, arrived off the West end of Bermuda June 12th.. They put to sea on the 16th, and next day took the sloop Anne, William BRAY master, from Honduras for Rotterdam, with mahogany, which is since arrived.

(218) Wilmington, August 23. On Thursday last arrived in this Port, the Letter of Marque Brigantine Resolution, belonging to this Part of the State, and commanded by Joseph MEREDITH; accompanied by a large Ship called the Polly, Capt. Thomas COLLART, bound to Jamaica from the Missisippi.. There is no Doubt of her being a Prize, and will sell to a considerable Amount, being well fitted, and loaded with a Cargo very suitable to the West India Market.

(219) Advertisements. August 25, 1777. To be Sold at Auction, on Wednesday the 24th of September next, at Black Creek, in Carteret County, The valuable and noted Saw Mill, one Half of a Grist Mill with bolting Cloths, and 400 Acres of Land, lately belonging to Henry STANTON, deceased. A full Tide flows to the Mill Tail, which lies about 14 Miles from Beaufort. At the same Time will be sold..Working Oxen, Log Carriage, Chains, &c., some planting Utensils, a good Set of Blacksmiths Tools,..Iron, a Set of Turners Tools, some Carpenters Tools, Cows and Calves, other Cattle and Horses, Household Furniture, Hives of Bees, a small Still, a swift sailing Boat with a Suit of Sails, and a great many Articles... Hope STANTON, Executrix.

(220) I am by Authority ordered to inform all Soldiers belong to Col. BAKER's Regiment of Horse for the state of Georgia, who have been so unfortunate as to desert the Service, that on their appearing to me in Wilmington, on or before the 10th Day of October next, they may be assured of a free Pardon, and good Usage, and no Reflections cast on them for being guilty of so disgraceful a Crime. Lee. DEKEYSER, Captain of Horse for the State of Georgia.

September 5, 1777. Number 392.

(221) Boston, July 24. By an express arrived here last Friday night from Manchester, in the State of Vermont which he left on Tuesday the 15th instant, we learn, that the enemy were then in possession of and fortifying Castle Town, on the Hampshire grants, so called, and cutting a road through towards South Bay, in order to get to Fort Ann; that there had been a battle at Hugbarton, between a body of our troops under the command of Colonel Ebenezer FRANCIS, of the Massachusetts State, and Col. HALE, of the Hampshire State, and about 2000 of the enemy, when our people retreated, being overpowered by numbers; that the loss on our side was reported to be about 150 killed and missing, among the former were the above mentioned Colonels FRANCIS and HALE...

(222) New-London, July 18. Last Saturday a prize was sent into port, taken by the sloop Trumbull, Capt. Henry BILLINGS, from this port.

(223) Hartford, July 28. Last week Major General PRESCOT, lately taken prisoner at Rhode Island, was brought under guard to East Windsor, where he is stationed, under the care of Captain Ebenezer GRANT.

(224) Fish-Kill, July 31. Extract of a letter from Moses's Creek, July 26. We have just had a brush with the enemy at Fort Edward, in which Lieutenant VAN VEIGHTEN was most inhumanly butchered and scalped ... They took a young woman, Janey M'CREA by name, out of a house at Fort Edward..killed and scalped her in cold blood...

(225) Philadelphia, August 6. A letter from Benjamin FRANKLIN and Silas DEANE, esquires, to Lord STORMONT the English ambassador at Paris... B. FRANKLIN.

(226) Williamsburg, August 22. ..In pursuance of the powers granted by Act of Assembly..the Governor..with the advice of the Council, appointed Thomas NELSON, jun. esq; county lieutenant of York, brigadier

(226) (Cont.) general and commander in chief of the forces in this commonwealth.

(227) Newbern, September 5, 1777. State of North Carolina. By his Excellency Richard CASWELL, Esquire, Governor, Captain General, and Commander in Chief, of the said State. A Proclamation. Whereas it will be difficult for the Inhabitants of this State to supply themselves with Common Salt, unless the Exportation and Transportation thereof be prohibited..issue this my Proclamation hereby prohibiting the Exportation and Transportation of Salt from this State after this date, untill the Expiration of thirty Days from the date hereof.. Given under my Hand, and Seal at Arms, at Newbern, the 2d Day of September, in the Year of our Lord 1777, and in the second Year of our Independence. Richard CASWELL. By his Excellency's Command, J. GLASGOW, Sec.

(228) Advertisements. To the Public, Attendance on the Assemblies for a Number of Years past, as their Clerk, and the frequent Meetings of the Congress and Councils of Safety as their Secretary..hath so much impaired my Health, that I shall be under the Necessity of resigning my present Appointment, as Clerk of the Senate, at the next Meeting... J. GREEN, jun. Sept. 1, 1777.

(229) To Be Sold on very reasonable terms, 1697 acres of land situate on the..river of Pee Dee in the county of Craven in South Carolina, bounded on the lands of John SAUNDERS, Esq; Mr. LAROACH and others..near the Cherraws court house... Also 400 acres situate in St. George's parish Berkly county..on the lands of Mr. PERMAIN, the heirs of Peter BACOT and others. The above tracts of land were part of the estate of Doctor Philip AYTON deceased..apply to Mr. James BALLANTINE merchant in Charles Town, or the subscriber in Newbern... James BALLANTINE (This name was corrected to that of James HAMILTON in the 12 September issue.)

(230) Newbern, Sept. 2d, 1777. Mr. Printer, Whereas some of the principal Officers formerly belonging to the Sturdy Beggar, then under my Command, has wontonly and cruelly spread and circulated scandalous and malicious Stories to the Prejudice of my Reputation... John M'KEEL. Newbern August 10, 1777. Capt. John M'KEEL, Dear Sir, We are very sorry to be informed by you that the Tongue of Slander has been busy with your Character..it is with great Pleasure we give our Testimony in your favour, and assure you that we are fully satisfied with your Courage and Conduct while you commanded the Sturdy Beggar of whom we are part Owners. We are Sir your obedient Servants, David STEWART. Daniel BOWLY.

September 12, 1777. Number 393.

(231) Philadelphia, August 22. (Letter) From General Philip SCHUYLER to The Hon. John HANCOCK, Esq.... Published by order of Congress, John HANCOCK, President.

(232) Advertisements. State of North-Carolina, Craven county, ss. To all sheriffs, constables, and others, liege subjects of the said state. Greeting. Whereas complaint hath been made to me, one of the

41

(232) (Cont.) Justices of the Peace for the said state, by John BRYAN, Esq; High Sheriff of the same, that last night the public gaol of the said county was broke open, and the following persons made their escape from thence, viz. Michael KELLY, an Irishman, for robbery. He is about 26 years of age, about 5 feet 6 inches high, had on a sea green coat and osnabrigs trousers, has lost one of his under teeth, and had a scar on his right cheek. Matthias FARNAN, for robbery. He is about 28 years of age, 5 feet 7 or 8 inches high, had on a dark coloured jacket, a chip hat, and has a sore on his leg. James RAWLINS, for high treason. He is a noted villain, and was one of the principals in the late conspiracy against the state, has lived for two years past in Martin county, and is very famous in the art of legerdemain; about 40 years of age, of a very black complection, and had a cut on one of his cheeks. The above named FARNAN and KELLY obtained a pass from Mr. TISDALE a few days before their commitment, which it is probable they will now make use of. These are therefore..to require you ..to make diligent search, by way of hue and cry... 9th September, 1777. Joseph LEECH. N. B. Whoever apprehends and secures the above persons..shall have 10 l. reward for RAWLINS and 5 l. for each of the other two, from John KENNEDY, Gaoler.

(233) To be Sold, at the plantation where Simon BRIGHT, Esq; late of Dobbs county, deceased, lately dwelt, at public vendue, on the third day of next October, Part of the personal estate of the deceased, consisting of a small library of books, several neat guns, a very good compass and chain for surveying land..negro slaves..horses..cattle, hogs, and sheep.... John COOKE, James BRIGHT, Executors.

(234) Newbern, Sept. 10, 1777. Committed to the public gaol, the 4th of this instant, a negro man named WILL, about 22 years of age, about 5 feet 7 or 8 inches high, speaks good English.. He says he belongs to John WOODBURY, near Georgetown, South Carolina, who bought him about last February from John RICE, on Roanoke. His owner is desired to apply for him and pay charges. John KENNEDY, Gaoler.

(235) Chowan county, August 30, 1777. Committed to the public gaol in Edenton, on the 28th of this instant, a negro man who says his name is JACOB, that he belonged to Thomas MC KNIGHT, and was sent to one of the back counties to the iron works, and run away from that place... Evan SKINNER, Sheriff.

September 19, 1777. Number 394.

(236) Fish-Kill, August 14. Hanover (New Jersey) August 6, 1777. Mr. LOUDON, I Take the freedom to inclose you a copy of a letter which I received through the hands of his Excellency General WASHINGTON. I beg the favour of you to publish it, with this letter. Indeed I..wish it to be published in all the states, that the people may see that every measure is adopted by our enemies to accomplish their tyrannical purposes... This letter was directed to me as commander at Ticonderoga.. I am, Sir, your most humble servant, John SULLIVAN. "Sir;... Your sincere friend, Peter LIVIUS, Montreal, June 2, 1777. To John SULLIVAN, Esquire." This letter was taken out of a canteen, with a false bottom, by General SCHUYLER, at Fort Edward, this 16th day of June, in the presence of Benjamin HICKS, Captain. Henry B. LIVINGSTON,

(236) (Cont.) A. D. C. to Gen. SCHUYLER. John W. WENDELL, Captain. John LANSING, jun. Secretary to Gen. SCHUYLER. I certify, upon honour that this letter was taken out of a canteen which I delivered to General SCHUYLER, which canteen I received from Col. VAN DYCK, who separated part of the wire from the false bottom to see whether it was the canteen I was sent for..taking out the letter..returned it into the canteen without breaking the seals. Bar. J. V. VALKENBURGH, Lieutenant.

(237) Extract of a letter from Albany, August 11. "..Last Wednesday, about 9 o'clock, an engagement ensued between a part of the militia of Tryon county, under the command of General HARKIMER and a party of savages, tories, and regulars, about halfway between Eriskie and Fort Stanwix. It lasted till three o'clock..when the enemy thought proper to retire, leaving General HARKIMER master of the field.. The enemy lost..some of their chief men, such as Joseph BRANDT, William JOHNSON, Peter JOHNSON (bastards of the late Sir William JOHNSON), Stephen WATTS, Johannes Jost HARKIMER (a brother to the General) and a number of others, Indians and regulars."

(238) Kingston, August 11. On Monday or Tuesday last passed through this town, Mr. John ADAMS, on express from Boston to Philadelphia...

(239) Advertisements. In Congress, August 6, 1777. The Committee of Treasury report, That they have conferred with the Managers of the States Lottery, and find..that from the present state of the lottery, and the uncertainty of the enemy's intentions..recommend the drawing to be postponed till the 6th day of November next... Copy from the Journals. William C. HOUSTON, Dept. Sec.

(240) Newbern, Sept. 17, 1777. Committed to the public gaol,..a negro man named CORK, belonging to Henry GOODMAN, of Dobbs county... John KENNEDY, Gaolor.

September 26, 1777. Number 395.

(241) Philadelphia, August 30. .. Sept. 2. James IRVINE, Esq; of this city (late Colonel of a Pennsylvania battalion in the continental army) is appointed a Brigadier General of this state.

(242) Philadelphia, Sept. 2. General SULLIVAN, with 1500 men, under Generals SMALLWOOD and BORIE, went from Morristown last Thursday fe'night at noon, crossed at Elizabeth town point, and was on Staten Island at day break the next morning. One party went towards New York.. the other went towards Amboy.. About 3 o'clock the rear guard of our army, consisting of 126 men, was attacked, and twice repulsed the assailants, who suffered much in killed, but our party having expended all their ammunition, were obliged to surrender; among which are Col. ANTILL, Major John STEWART, of Maryland, a Major of Col. HAZEN's regiment..and others..

(243) Head Quarters, August 25, 1777. Sir, A Messenger is just arrived with the enclosed letters from General ARNOLD and Col. GANSEVOORT... I am, Sir,..Horatio GATES. His Excellency John HANCOCK, Esq; President of Congress. Fort SCHUYLER, August 22, 1777. Dear Sir

(243) (Cont.) ... About 7 o'clock this evening Hanjort SCHUYLER arrived here, and informed me that Gen. ARNOLD with 2000 men were on their march for this post... I am.., Peter GANSEVOORT, Colonel. Mohawk river, ten miles above Fort Daton, August 23, 1777. Five o'clock P. M. Dear General, I wrote you the 21st instant from the German Flats.. I shall immediately detach about 900 men, and make a forced march to the fort... Your affectionate obedient humble servant, B. ARNOLD. Hon. Major Gen. GATES. ... Published by order of Congress. Charles THOMSON, Sec'ry.

(244) Newbern, Sept. 26. Last Week a very melancholy Accident happened at Core-Sound. Mr. Richard BLACKLEDGE, of this County, who was carrying on the Public Salt Works of this State, was unfortunately drowned in crossing over from the Town of Beaufort to the Salt Works on New-Port River.. After condoling with his disconsolate Widow, and numerous and amiable Family, on the Loss of so tender a Husband and Parent, we are next to view him in a Public Character, and deplore his Loss as a public Misfortune.

(245) By a Gentleman just arrived from Charles-Town..one of the large three decked Ships lately carried in there by Capt. BIDDLE in the Randolph continental Frigate proves to be a Prize taken by Capt. PALMER in the Privateer Nancy, belonging to Mr. John W. STANLY of this Town.

(246) Strayed from the Subscriber living in Newbern, on Friday the 12th of September, a small sorrel Horse..he formerly belonged to Mr. John HAMILTON, and is supposed to be gone toward Halifax... Henry VIPON.

October 3, 1777. Number 396.

(247) Philadelphia, Sept. 2. Mr. DUNLAP, Please to publish the two following Letters.. Ar. ST. CLAIR. Philadelphia, August 30, 1777. Sir, ... Ar. ST. CLAIR. (to) The Hon. Major General SULLIVAN. Philadelphia, August 30, 1777. Sir, .. John SULLIVAN (to) The Hon. Major General ST. CLAIR.

(248) Philadelphia, Sept. 2. James IRVIN, Esq; of this city, (late Colonel of a Pennsylvania battalion in the continental Army,) is appointed a Brigadier General of this State.

(249) In Congress, June 14, 1777. Resolved, That the Flag of the United States be Thirteen Stripes alternate red and white; that the Union be Thirteen Stars white in a blue field, representing a new constellation. Extract from the Minutes. Charles THOMSON, Secretary.

(250) August 28. Congress proceeded to the election of the Committee to collect evidence and facts relative to the evacuation of Ticonderoga, &c. and the ballots being taken, Mr. LAURENS, Mr. Richard Henry LEE and Mr. John ADAMS, were elected. Published by order of Congress, Charles THOMSON, Secretary.

(251) Advertisements. In the Press, And next Week will be Published, The Acts of the last Session of Assembly, held at Newbern in April last. Mr. PINKNEY, who was appointed Printer to this State in April

(251) (Cont.) last, being dead, and no Prospect of the State's being able to get their Laws printed, Mr. DAVIS..has undertaken this necessary Work, and will dispatch them to the several Counties as soon as possible.

(252) A List of Letters remaining in the Post-Office, Newbern, viz. Capt. Stephen STIMPSON, 1 Letter, received 6th April last. Mr. James FEREBEE, 1 do. 11th May, Mr. John ETHEREGE, 1 do. 9th June. Col. William DAVIS, 1 do. 16th June, Mr. John HOUSE, 1 do. 7th July. Mr. Lemuel CRAVATH, 3 do. 4, 11, 18 Aug. Mr. John BRYAN, 1 do. 23d Aug. Hannah BRAN, to care of Mr. John BRYAN, 1 do. 23d do. Capt. Cornelius ANNIBLE, 1 do. 1st Sept. Capt. Thomas KILL, 1 do. do. Capt. Francis HODGSON, 1 do. 8th do. Capt. William BIGELOW, 1 do. 15th do. Mr. John HARRIS, Swift's Creek, 1 do. 22d do. Capt. William SPAIGHT, 1 do. do. Mrs. Elizabeth DAWSON, 1 do. do. William CARRAWAY, Esq; 1 do. 29th do. Mr. Joseph HADY, 1 do. do. The persons to whom these letters are directed..are desired to pay the postage, and take up the same. Some of them may be of consequence, and require to be answered by post again, which shall be punctually sent to any post-office in the united states, by Their humble servant, R. COGDELL, Postmaster.

(253) Beaufort County, October 1, 1777. Taken up by the Subscriber, the 17th of September last, a Negro Fellow who calls himself SAM, 4 Feet 10 Inches high, about 45 Years of Age, his upper Teeth filed sharp, and has several Guiney Marks about his Body... Charles LEATH.

October 10, 1777. Number 397.

(254) Philadelphia. Sept. 6. (Letter) Chad's Ford, Sept. 11, 1777, 5 o'clock P. M. Sir, ... Robert H. HARRISON. (to) The Hon. John HANCOCK, Esquire. (Letter) Chester, Sept. 11, 1777, 12 o'clock at night. Sir, I am sorry to inform you that in this day's engagement we have been obliged to leave the enemy masters of the field. ..the enemy attacked..the division..under the command of General WAYNE and the light troops under General MAXWELL; who, after a severe conflict, also retired. The militia, under..General ARMSTRONG, being posted at a ford about two miles below Chad's, (Chad's Ford, on the Brandywine) had no opportunity of engaging.. The Marquis LA FAYETTE was wounded in the leg, and General WOODFORD in the hand... G. WASHINGTON. Published by order of Congress. Charles THOMSON, Sec'ry.

(255) Extract of a letter from Philadelphia, dated Sept. 13, 1777, 9 o'clock. "I saw General MAXWELL at Chester; he..with 500 men, crossed early in the morning over the Brandywine and laid in ambush for the enemy..and left 400 of them dead in the field.. Not one Maryland officer was killed; Capt. Joseph FORD, was wounded in the arm."

(256) Williamsburg, Sept. 26. Copy of a letter from the Governor of Maryland to his Excellency the Governor, dated Baltimore, Thursday 1 o'clock, Sept. 18, 1777. Sir, The last of the enemy's fleet have just passed the mouth of this river, and we suppose are..under orders for Delaware.. General WASHINGTON's head quarters are at the City Tavern, in Philadelphia..your..servant, Thomas JOHNSON. (to) Governor HENRY.

(257) Charles-Town, September 11. On Saturday last John MAC QUEEN,

(257) (Cont,) Exq; of this place, who went a volunteer with Capt. BIDDLE, came up to town in the Randolph's boat, and brought us accounts..that..they took two ships and two brigs..a small sloop.. The other ship is the Severn, Capt. James HENDERSON, from Jamaica for London.. One brig is the Charming Peggy, Capt. Philip LYON...

(258) Baltimore, Sept. 23, 1777. A Gentleman just arrived from Camp informs, that General WASHINGTON crossed over the Scuylkill on Friday Night, with four divisions of his army, and are now encamped near Swede's Ford, in front of the enemy, lying on this side of Scuylkill. Generals WANE, MAXWELL, and the militia under Gen. POTTER, in the rear of the enemy, whose camp is at the Valley Forge, about 5 or 6 miles from the Swede's Ford. General SMALLWOOD, with 2500 of the Maryland militia, joined Gen. WANE on Sunday Morning, all in high spirits.

(259) Advertisements. To be Rented for the term of one year,..the last Saturday of this instant, and to be entered on the 1st of November next, The two plantations on Otter creek the south side of Neuse, belonging to the heir of George P. LOVICK, deceased. Also..the plantation on Trent now in possession of John FOY...by the Guardian.

October 17, 1777.

(260) Advertisements. For Sale by the Subscriber, on Coor Creek, near Newbern, Two Waggons..Team of Horses..also a very fine full blooded Gelding. Wm. BRYAN. October 14, 1777.

October 24, 1777. Number 399.

(261) Baltimore, Sept. 29, 1777. By his Excellency William HOWE, &c. A Declaration to the Inhabitants of Pennsylvania, the Lower Counties on Delaware, and the Counties on the Eastern Shore of Maryland. Sir William HOWE..doth hereby assure the inhabitants..that..he hath issued the strictest orders to the troops, for the preservation of regularity and good discipline... By his Excellency's command, Robert M'KENSIE.

(262) New-Castle, ss. This day came Francis ALEXANDER, a reputable resident in the county aforesaid, before me..a justice of the peace, made oath, that he was eye witness to several brutal ravages committed by the merciless troops of the tyrant of Great-Britain..that he saw one of them..ravish, or attempt violently to effect a rape on the person of a young woman of spotless character, living at his house, notwithstanding her cries and resistance to the contrary... Francis ALEXANDER. Sworn before me this 31st Aug. 1777. Geo. LATIMER. The above deposition, taken in the presence of Wm. MAXWELL, Brigadier, Alexander MARTIN, Colonel, and Theo. BLAND, Colonel of a regiment of light dragoons.

(263) Lancaster, in Pennsylvania. Fresh and important intelligence, just arrived from the northern army. Kingston, Tuesday 9 o'clock A. M. 23d of September..intelligence from the Secretary of the committee of Albany, by letters of which the following are copies, viz. Camp 4 miles above Stillwater, Sept. 20, 1777. Dear Sir, General GATES being extremely hurried, has desired me to answer your letter of this day...

(263) (Cont.) I am, dear Sir, &c. James WILKINSON. Albany, Sept. 21, 1777, 7 o'clock A. M. Dear Sir, I Was last night favoured with a letter from the Adjutant General, of which that on the other side is a copy... Dr. POTTS..farther informs that it is believed at our camp we are in possession of Ticonderoga.. We had some brave officers killed, such as Colonels COBURN and ADAMS.. Major FISCH of Cortlandts has a slight wound.. Yours sincerely, Mat. VISSCHER. Mr. YATES. Camp above Stillwater, Sept. 22, 1777. Sir,... Your most obedient Servant, Udney HAY. John BARCLAY, Esq. Albany, Sept. 21, 1777. Dear Sir, Since writing mine of this day's date, I have seen Capt. Jacob J. LANSINGH, assistant deputy muster master..our troops were in possession of Ticonderoga... Yours sincerely, Matt. VISSCHER. Monday morning, 6 o'clock. Dear Sir,... I am, Sir,... Horatio GATES.

(264) Newbern, October 24, 1777. On Tuesday last was married, Mr. James GREEN, Jun. of this County, to Miss Peggy COGDELL, second Daughter of Colonel Richard COGDELL, of this Town; a most amiable and agreeable young Lady, with a considerable Share of Beauty and other Accomplishments.

(265) Newbern, October 21, 1777. Whereas by sundry Acts of the Assembly of the State of Georgia, the following Encouragement is given to such Persons as will come and settle in the said State, viz. 500 Acres of Land for every Head of a Family, and 50 Acres for every white Person belonging to the same, and also 50 Acres for each Negro, not exceeding 10 in number.. There are also two Battalions of Minute Men now raising, to continue for two Years. The above Bounty in Land is given, and also a Bounty of 30 Dollars in Money, and 20 Pence Sterling per Day, with the same Rations of Provisions as the continental Troops for the Privates. These Battalions will be stationed on the western Frontiers of the State, where the Lands are granted... Joseph WOOD, Edward LANGWORTHY, Continental Delegates.

(266) October 15, 1777. To be Sold at public vendue, at the late dwelling-house of Richard BLACKLEDGE, Esq; deceased, on Tuesday the 4th of November next, Three Negro Slaves..Horses, Cattle, Sheep and Hogs..a new Copper Distill and Lead Worm..and in Newbern, at Mr. John GREEN's store, a quantity of Bar Iron and Rods for Nails..Soal Leather, Saddle and upper Leather,..and part of a Stock of Cattle at Pecoson Point... Jacob BLOUNT, Christopher NEALE, Richard BLACKLEDGE, Spyers SINGLETON, Executors.

October 31, 1777. Number 400.

(267) Extract of a letter from a member of Congress, dated York, October 10, 1777. "On the 4th instant, our army made a wise and well concerted attack upon the British force, encamped at and near German-Town;..the enemy lost Gen. AGNEW, Colonels ABERCROMBIE, WALCOTT, BYRD of Virginia, and Gen. DE HEISTER's son killed, Gen. KNIPHAUSEN wounded in the hand.. On our part, General NASH is dead of his wounds, Col. HENDRICKS and Lieut. Col. PARKER from Virginia, wounded, but not mortally; two of General SULLIVAN's Aids mortally wounded, Colonel STONE of Maryland wounded, not mortally."

(268) Extract of a letter from York town, Pennsylvania, dated October

47

(268) (Cont.) 8, 1777.. This moment an express arrived, with a letter from Captain William PIERCE, dated Skippack camp, 12 o'clock P.M.
the day on which the above bloody battle was fought...General NASH is
mortally wounded with a cannon ball. Col. HENDRICKS is wounded below
the left eye, but likely to recover..Lieut. Col. PARKER, of the second
Virginia regiment, a brave officer, got wounded in the leg, and it is
said the bone is broke. Col. Matthew SMITH, our deputy adjutant general, got his leg broke by a grape shot. Cornet BAYLOR, of the light
horse, had one half of his foot shot away. Major JAMESON had his
horse killed under him, but he..was unhurt. Capt. DICKINSON was
slightly wounded in the knee. Capt. Thomas EDMONDS was so badly wounded that he died in a few hours. Capt. EUSTACE, of the first Virginia
regiment, was killed dead on the spot. Two Maryland Colonels, of the
name of STONE, were wounded..Col. J siah PARKER behaved like a hero.
Brigade Major SCOTT does honour to his country...

(269) Boston, September 11. Tuesday last, arrived at a safe port,
from a cruize, the ship Oliver Cromwell, Seth HARDING, Esq; commander,
with a prize ship... Same day arrived at the same port, a prize brig,
laden with oyl, &c. taken by the Tartar, Capt. James GRIMES. Capt.
BUNKER from Machias informs that on Thursday the 28th ult. three of
the enemy's frigates, with a brig ; commanded by the noted DAWSON,
paid a visit to that place.. Our loss was only one, Mr. James FOSTER
killed, and Mr. Jonas FARNSWORTH wounded, tho' not dangerous.

Thursday last arrived at a safe port the richest prize, tis said,
taken during the war..by Capt. John LEE of Newbury Port.

(270) Newbern, October 31, 1777. In the late Battle of Germantown,
fighting under the illustrious WASHINGTON, in the glorious Cause of
Freedom..fell the brave, but unfortunate Brigadier General NASH..how
severe must be the Stroke on his mournful and widowed Lady, who, with
two tender Infants..are left to lament his Loss...

(271) On Saturday last, sailed from this Port, on an intended Voyage
to Jamaica, a second Scotch Transport, having on Board a Number of
Gentlemen of that Nation, particularly Mess. ARCHIBALD and John HAMIL-
TON, Gentlemen that have long resided in America, and, with great Reputation, acquired very considerable Fortunes...

Supplement to the North-Carolina Gazette, Nov. 7, 1777.

(272) Newbern, November 8, 17 7. Last Night we received a Virginia
Paper, containing a Confirmation of the most pleasing and important
Account of the Surrender of General BURGOYNE, with his whole Army, to
Major General GATES...

(273) Extract of a letter from Baltimore, Tuesday morning, Oct. 23,
1777. "Jesse HOLLINGSWORTH came home last evening from Elk. He
brings an account that the enemy have certainly abandoned Wilmington
and gone on board their transports...."

(274) (Letter to) Lieutenant General BURGOYNE, Saratoga, Oct. 12,
1777. Sir, .. Your friend, Sir Francis CLARKE, by the information
of Doctor POTTS, the Director General of my hospital, languishes under

(274) (Cont.) a very dangerous wound.. At the solicitation of Major
WILLIAMS, I am prevailed upon to offer him and Major MEIBORM, in exchange for Col. Ethan ALLEN... I am, ..Horatio GATES.

November 7, 1777. Number 401.

(275) Annapolis, October 16. Extract of a letter from Trenton, October 7, 1777. "Last night a young Lady arrived here from Philadelphia..by her We have the following good consequences of the action of
the 4th instant.. General AGNEW was killed on the spot, and General
GRANT mortally wounded.. Rooms were engaged at Mrs. YARD's for six;
that it would take all our hospitals, and some other houses, to contain the wounded..the tories cry they must leave the city with General HOWE. Mrs. KEARSLEY has received Dr. SHIPPEN's house, as a reward for services done. Mrs. HOUSE and ____ are ordered out of your's
and Mr. DICKENSON's, which are to be given away to some of the faithful..."

(276) Baltimore, Oct. 14, 1777. Extract of a letter from camp,
dated 5th of October. The night before last our army marched in order
to attack the enemy.. I believe 14 miles.. The General himself, with
SULLIVAN's, SURLING's, and WAYNE's divisions, and NASH's brigade,
composed the centre; General CONWAY commanded the advance; GREEN, M'
DOUGALL, SMALLWOOD, and FERMOY, were to engage the enemy's right,
ARMSTRONG, with the militia, composed our right. Unluckily the wings
were not up in time.. The fogginess of the morning was very much a-
gainst us..in Germantown..they took possession of the houses..one
party from Mr. CHEW's house was very troublesome..General NASH had
his thigh shattered with a cannon ball, and must die (he is since
dead) Colonel STONE is shot through the ankle, Col. HALL bruised, Colonel HENDRICKS..is wounded in the head, but not dangerously. Jack
WHITE, who behaved bravely, I am afraid, is gone. Capt. COX is killed. Young BAYLOR was struck on the instep with a 4 pound ball..he
will lose his leg.

(277) Williamsburg, October 24. Extract of a letter from an officer
at camp, dated October 7, 1777. "The 9th regiment is lost; Col. MAT-
THEWS wounded, Col. SEARS killed; that Majors DARK, TOWLES, and SCOTT
wounded and taken, Major CAMPBELL wounded but brought off; General
NASH and Capt. SPOTIWO_D are dead of their wounds."

(278) Newbern, November 7, 1777. Extract of a Letter from the Chairman of the Committee of Albany, to the President of the Council of the
State of New York. "Last Night, at 8 o'Clock, the Capitulation, where
by General BURGOYNE and his whole Army surrendered themselves Prisoners of War, was signed; and this Morning they are to march out towards
the River about Fish Creek, with the Honours of War, and there ground
their Arms, from whence they are to be marched to the Massachusetts
Government."

November 14, 1777. Number 402.

(279) Head Quarters, Williamsburg, October 30, 1777. A Feu de joy
this afternoon at 3 o'clock, on the confirmation of the glorious news
of General BURGOYNE and his army being prisoners of war, all the troo

(279) (Cont.) are to parade at the barracks, the artillery with 13 discharges, the infantry with 3 rounds;..they will proceed..to Mr. POWELL's, where they will march in platoons round the capitol up the main street, to the common behind the court-house, there the battalion will be formed, and the firing begin; 13 discharges of cannon will be made, under the command of Capt. DE LA PORTE of the artillery... Edward CARRINGTON, L. C. A.

(280) State of North-Carolina. By his Excellency Richard CASWELL, Esq; Governor, Captain-General, and Commander in Chief of the State. A Proclamation. Whereas I have received authenticated Intelligence that General BURGOYNE, and the whole Army under his Command, after repeated Losses, surrendered themselves Prisoners of War to General GATES on the Fourteenth Day of October last..I have thought proper, with the Advice of the Council of State, to issue this Proclamation appointing Friday the Twenty Eighth Day of this Instant to be observed in all Churches and Congregations in this State as a Day of General and Solemn Thanksgiving..at Newbern, the Eighth Day of November in the Second Year of the Independence of the said State. Richard CASWELL. By his Excellency's Command. J. GLASGOW, Secretary of the State.

November 21, 1777. Number 403.

(281) New Windsor, Oct. __ (to) Gen. PUTNAM. Dear General, In consequence of a severe tartar emetic, which I ordered to be given the spy, I have in my possession a small silver bullet, from which I have taken a letter from CLINTON to BURGOYNE, of which the enclosed is an exact copy. With esteem, I am dear General, your obedient servant, Geo. CLINTON, Fort Montgomery, Oct. 8, 1777. (to) Gen. BURGOYNE. Nous y voici and nothing now between us but GATES... Faithfully your's, H. CLINTON.

(282) Advertisements. Taken up, at the mouth of Bay river, in Craven county, the 4th of this instant (November) a negro man, who says his name is WILL, about 30 years of age, about 6 feet high, has a mark in his forehead imitating a diamond, a circle round each eye (supposed to be his country mark)..and says he belongs to Mr. HARDY... John RIGGS.

November 28, 1777. Number 404.

(283) In Congress, November 1, 1777... It is therefore recommended to the legislative and executive powers of these United States, to set apart Thursday the 18th day of December next for Solemn Thanksgiving and Praise..of their Divine Benefactor... Extract from the minutes, Charles THOMSON, Sec'ry.

(284) Intelligence from Red-Bank. (to) His Excellency Gen. WASHINGTON. Red-Bank, October 23d, 1777... Am your Excellency's most obedient, and very humble servant, John HAZELWOOD.

(285) Red-Bank, 23d October, 1777. Sir,... I am, with the greatest respect, your Excellency's most obedient humble servant, Sam. WARD. 2 o'clock, Red-Bank, Oct. 23, 1777. Sir,... I have the honour to be, &c. Robert BALLARD.

(286) Newbern, November 28, 1777. By a Vessel 13 Days from the West Indies to our Bar, advices are received that the sloop Lydia, Capt. APPLETON, of 12 carriage guns and 50 men, fitted out by Mr. John W. STANLY of this Town, had taken and carried into Guadaloupe, a large Ship...

(287) Yesterday died at his House in this Town, after a very tedious and severe Illness, which he bore with great fortitude, Mr. Edward BATCHELOR, a Gentleman of singular Hospitality and Benevolence of Heart, and much respected in the Circle of his Acquaintance.

(288) State of North Carolina. In the House of Commons, 20th November, 1777. Whereas in the present critical situation of the American contest, it would be dishonourable to this State, highly injurious to the public service..that the officers of the troops raised as the Quota of this State for the continental army should quit their posts .. This House therefore do,..resolve and declare, that all and every officer..who shall, unless for good and sufficient reasons certified to the governor to be such by the Commander in Chief of the continental army, resign his commission at this critical period, shall be held..incapable of holding hereafter any office civil or military in the gift of this State..a copy of this be forwarded by..the Governor, to General WASHINGTON, and that it also be published in the News-Papers of this and the neighbouring States. A. NASH, S. C. John HUNT, C. H. C., By order, In the Senate, November 20th, 1777. Read and concurred with. S. ASHE, S. S.

(289) Advertisements. To be Sold, The following Tracts of good Land viz. One whole survey of 640 acres on Ellis's lake, within 18 miles of Newbern, in Carteret County.. 1500 acres, or upwards, in the fork of Brice's creek, Craven county. - 450 acres on the North side of Neuse river. - 200 acres adjoining the last mentioned tract, on the high road from Newbern to Halifax, 28 miles from the former. - One half a water lot in Beaufort, Carteret county, adjoining where Mr. James PARRAT now lives. - And three half acre lots, No. 70, 126, and 132, in Martinborough, Pitt county. - ..particulars by applying to Dr. HASLEN, or Mr. OGDEN, merchant in Newbern, or to the proprietor in Bertie county. W. BRIMAGE.

(290) Newbern, November 19, 1777. Strayed or stolen from this Town. a black horse.. Whoever will deliver the said horse at Mr. WRENFORD': or Mr. David THOMSON, in this Town, shall be paid five pounds reward. Thomas TURNER.

(291) Newbern, November 24th, 1777. Ten Dollars reward. Lost out of a back chamber at Mr. Edmond WRENFORD's the 22d instant, a chased pint silver bowl, marked on the side I. T. W. in a cypher, whoever will deliver said bowl to Mrs. WRENFORD, shall receive the above reward and no questions asked. John WHITE.

(292) Newbern, November 28th, 1777. Strayed away from Newbern..a black horse.. Whoever delivers the said horse to me in Newbern, shal have 20 shillings. James LITTLE.

(293) Bath-Town, North-Carolina, Nov. 18. As I am left in this Stat

(293) (Cont.) on the recruiting service, and have charge of the recruiting officers belonging to the 5th Battalion, desire they will
meet me at William BROWN's in Bath, on the 5th day of December next,..
with the recruits and deserters.. I also order all soldiers belonging
to the said battalion.,sick or on furlow with the deserters to meet
at said place and day, that I may be able to make a just return of
that part of our regiment left in this state. Ben. STEDMAN.

December 5, 1777. Number 405.

(294) Lancaster, November 1. We are assured from York-town, where
Congress now sit, that Indian affairs at no time, were in a more pro-
mising way. Through the interposition of Congress, RATTLE-TRAP and
TURKEY'S TAIL were sent by numerous tribes of the southern Indians to
their northern brethren. Gen. SCHUYLER had advised that 140 of them
had joined Gen. GATES... This last circumstance had doubtless been
in consequence of the important blow given the savages near fort
Schuyler, by the brave, but unfortunate Gen. HERKIMER, who headed the
intripid militia of New-York State, and of the..victory..by the formidable militia of New-Hampshire, led by that hardy soldier, Gen.
STARK, assisted by the gallant Colonels WARNER, BROWN, and some continental troops.

(295) A Proclamation. By his Excellency George WASHINGTON, Esq; General and Commander in Chief of the Forces of the United States of America. Whereas sundry soldiers, belonging to the armies of the said
States, have deserted from the same;..to all those who have so offend-
ed, and who shall return to their respective corps..before the first
day of January next, that they shall obtain a full and free pardon...
24th day of October, Anno Domini 1777. G. WASHINGTON. By his Excellency's command, Robt. HARRISON, Sec.

(296) Newbern, Dec. 1st, 1777. To the end that deserters may have
an opportunity of availing themselves of the pardon offered by the
above proclamation..I have been ordered into this State for the express purpose of apprehending and receiving all deserted soldiers..
I hereby give notice that every deserted soldier from the continental
troops, who shall surrender himself to me at Kingston, in Dobbs County
..before the first day of January next, will be entitled to pardon..
a reward of ten dollars for each deserter, after that time. William
CASWELL, Capt. 5th N. Carolina battalion.

December 12, 1777. Number 406.

(297) Fish-Kill, October 23. Last Thursday one TAYLOR, a spy, was
hanged at Hurley, who was detected with a letter to BURGOYNE. Last
Monday our people took a small schooner belonging to the enemy, in the
north river, near Rhynebeck... Nicholas JAMES and George HOPKINS, two
of the New-York pilots, were taken on board. We learn that the enemy
have burnt the house of the late judge LIVINGSTON, the house of Mr.
Robert LIVINGSTON, and sundry others.

(298) From the Pennsylvania Ledger of November 6, printed at Philadelphia by James HUMPHREYS, jun. Philadelphia, Nov. 5. Copy of a letter from..Gen. BURGOYNE, to..Sir William HOWE, K. B.

(299) Camp at Saratoga, October 14, 1777. At a general court-mar-
tial held at Perkiomy, in Pennsylvania, by order of his Excellency
General WASHINGTON, on the 7th day of October, 1777, and by adjourn-
ment, on the 10th of the same month, Goodrich CRUMP, of the state of
Virginia, a captain in the 1st Virginia regiment, charged with cowardice, was tried, found guilty of that crime in the action of the 4th
of October, at Germantown, and sentenced therefore to be cashiered,
and to have his name, place of abode, and punishment, published in
the news-papers in and about the camp, and in..the particular State
he came from..; after which it should be deemed scandalous for any
officer to associate with him... Timothy PICKERING, Adj. Gen. Head
Quarters, October 24.

(300) Newbern, December 12, 1777. The Printer of the London Gazette,
since the American War, has been thought the greatest Liar on Earth,
but Messrs. Hugh GAINE and James RIVINGTON, of New-York, Printers,
far exceed their more respectable Brethren in England, in this curious
Art.

(301) On Tuesday last was married, Mr. Waitstill AVERY, of Mecklenburg County, to Mrs. FRANCKS, Widow of the late Mr. Edward FRANCKS,
of this County.

(302) Advertisements. Halifax, December 10. I Have still on hand,
belonging to the estate of Joseph MONTFORD, deceased, sundry tracts
of land..which I will sell cheap for ready money or short credit viz.
about 6000 acres in the county of Tryon, 370 acres in Orange county,
near Hillsborough, about 6000 acres in Bute county, in different parts
thereof, about 1500 acres in Halifax county, also sundry other small
tracts in different parts of this state.. All persons who have any
demands against the said estate, are desired to make them known on or
before the first day of May next, as I propose to make a division of
the said estate on that day... Henry MONTFORD, Executor.

(303) Hertford-County, Dec. 1st. Sixty Dollars reward, For apprehending five deserters belonging to the 2d North-Carolina battalion
of continental troops, viz. Roger MURPHY who passed for an English-man
about 35 years of age five feet six or seven inches high, a thick and
well made person, short lightish hair. Lewis SIMONS a French-man
about five feet seven inches high. John LAPLANTY, a French-man five
feet 9 inches high, pretty thick and well made, light hair. John
Battice FROMENTIER a French-man..about five feet five inches high, 23
years of age, slim made, of a sworthy complexion, long dark hair..the
above reward or 12 dollars for each. Sam. JONES.

(304) December 12, 1777. Ran away from the subscriber, a negro fellow... Everitt HOUSE.

(305) On Friday the 19th December next, pursuant to the Will of Mr.
Edward BATCHELOR, deceased, will be sold by public Vendue, at the
stores of said BATCHELOR, A quantity of dry goods..a small sloop and
schooner..as they now lay at the wharf of said BATCHELOR. And on
Thursday the 8th January next will be sold, Three quarters of the
Ship Harmony Hall as she now lies at Mr. CORNELL's wharf.. At the
same time will be sold a half share of the schooner Polly-burthen

(305) (Cont.) about 95 tons... Thomas HASLEN, Executor. Frances BATCHELOR, Executrix.

(306) December 4, 1777. To be sold on Tarr-River at the house of the subscriber just below Col. SIMPSON's..on the 1st and 2d day of January next..corn, cattle,..sheep..rice, a new desk and Mohogony tea-table, a dining table, and kitchen tables, two pair fire-dogs, chairs, bed steads,.flander flax seed, bonny vess beens, cotton.. cyder barrels, some books of law and divinity..also about 650 acres of very good land with a large plantation..about 1400 young bearing peach trees, and 250 apple trees..a dwelling house 24 by 16 feet, a kitchen 16 by 12, a milk-house 12 by 8, a smoak-house 12 feet square, and corn crib, the place is well attended with springs, it joins great Contentny creek and Nauhunte swamp, above Col. SHEPHERD's in Dobbs County..and joins Richard HODGES's, upon wheat swamp, about eight miles from Neuse-river above Kingston in Dobbs. The above lands I would sell cheap for the money, as I propose moving very shortly into the South Province. Frederick GIBBLE.

December 26, 1777. Number 408.

(307) Williamsburg, Dec. 12. We learn from the northern papers, that a Mr. John BROWN has lately made his appearance (without a flag, or even a pass) at York in Pennsylvania, who says he was sent by Mr. WILLING of Philadelphia with a verbal message from General HOWE to Congress..he was sent a prisoner to Lancaster, and by order of the Council of Pennsylvania, committed to the common jail.

(308) London, October 2. Extract of a letter from Mr. Izrael POWLEY, dated at Cadiz, September 8, 1777...

(309) Newbern, December 26. On Wednesday last the General Assembly of this State, finished the Business of the Session, having passed 48 Bills..particularly a Bill for establishing Courts of Law, and a Bill for opening the Land Office, and granting the vacant Lands in this State.. The Honourable Samuel ASHE, Samuel SPENCER, and James IRE-DELL, Esqrs. are appointed Judges of the supreme Courts of this District, and Waitstill AVERY, Esq; is appointed Attorney General for the State.

(310) Advertisements. Newbern, December 20, 1777. Whereas it hath pleased his Excellency Richard CASWELL, Esq; Governor, &c. of this State, to order a Court of Enquiry to be held by the continental Officers under my Command, to take into Consideration the Petition of sundry Persons, who are or were Soldiers in the continental Army raised in this State, and suggest they have Served the Time for which they were inlisted, and from whom Discharges are withheld: Therefore I hereby desire all Officers now within this State that are on the continental Establishment, to meet me at Newbern the 7th of January next, to hold the..Court; at which Place all those who think they are intitled to Discharges, are also desired to attend. John LUTTRILL. December 20, 1777.

(311) Newbern, December 24. By virtue of a resolve made at Newbern by the Assembly at their last session, will be sold by public vendue,

(311) (Cont.) at Wilmington, the 17th of February next. The armed
Brigantine Washington, with her guns, stores, tackle, apparrel and
furniture... William HOOPER, Hen. TOOMER, Commissioners.

(312) Beaufort, Dec. 1st. Taken up by the subscriber, a negro fellow
about middle age, 5 feet 6 inches high, of a yellowish complexion..his
teeth are filed and has lost three toes of his right foot..he says
his name is WILL... Charles LEITH.

(313) Dobbs-County, Dec. 18. Ran away from the subscriber October
last, a negro fellow named DICK, about 5 feet 8 inches high, a new
negro, has three toes of the right foot cut off..much marked with his
country marks, since he ran away he was taken up by John RIGGS on Bay
river, and said his name was WILL. Whoever delivers him to me in
Dobbs or to Mr. David THOMSON in Newbern, shall receive 3 pounds reward. Everitt HOUSE.

1778 - Filmed from originals in the University of North Carolina
Library-The following issues missing-February 27, March 20, April 17,
October 23, 30, December 7 through 28.

January 2, 1778. Number 409.

(314) Newbern, Jan. 2. The following Bills were passed at the General Assembly lately held at the Palace in Newbern.. An act for al-
tering the name of John GILLIARD to the name of John ISLER...

(315) Baltimore, Dec. 9, 1777. Extract of a letter from General
GATES, dated Albany Nov. 16... "I take it for granted, that General
PUTNAM and General George CLINTON acquainted your Excellency, that the
enemy abandoned all their forts and posts upon the North River, the
23d ult. and retreated to New-York; and that fort Independence, near
Kingsbridge, is also evacuated and destroyed."... Published by order
of Congress. Charles THOMSON, Sec'ry.

(316) In the House of Delegates, Williamsburg, December 10. Resolved,
that the governor and Council in draughting a detachment of the militia of this Commonwealth, and marching it to head quarters, in the
neighbouring State of Pennsylvania, actually invaded by a foreign
enemy, have acted according to the laws of this Commonwealth. John
TAZEWELL, C. H. D. December 17, 1777. Agreed to by the Senate. J.
BECKLEY, C. S.

(317) Williamsburg, Dec. 19. Extract of a letter from a gentleman
in the Northern Neck, dated December 15, 1777. "I arrived last night
from Potowmack, where I have been stationed 10 days. We have hitherto
prevented the enemy getting fresh provisions from our shore, but many
Negroes have gone off to them.. Capt. Townsend DADE had his batteau
drawn up and locked in his barn. The night following 10 negroes took
his oxen, broke open the door, carried her back to the river, and ef-
fected their escape. The sufferers..were Mr. FITZHUGH of Chatham,
three fellows, one wench, and four children; Mr. FITZHUGH of Marmion,
one fellow; Colonel Henry FITZHUGH, five fellows; Major STITH, three
fellows; Henry FITZHUGH, one fellow; Thacker WASHINGTON, two fellows;
Mr. MOXLEY, one wench. I was charged with a flag from Colonel SKISKER

(317) (Cont.) to endeavour a recovery of those negroes...

(318) Williamsburg, Dec. 19. Postscript of a letter, dated Sunday evening, York-town, Dec. 7. On Saturday the 15th of November 1777, died, near Germantown, Capt. James FOSTER, of the 15th Virginia regiment. If ever military ardour and patriotic zeal deserved an eulogium, it may, with truth be said, to be due this brave and gallant officer: Ye patriots, ye have lost a friend; Ye soldiers, ye have lost a Brother.

(319) Our Readers are desired to correct an Error of the Press, which passed unnoticed in our last, where, in the Newbern Paragraph, the Judges were said to be appointed for this District, which should have been, for this State.

(320) Advertisements. Chesterfield in Virginia, Dec. 20, 1777. For sale, and now stands at the subscribers plantation at the Falls of James River, Chesterfield county, in the state of Virginia, The two noted stud horses, viz. Regulus..and Ranter... William BLACK.

January 9, 1778. Number 410.

(321) Roseau, Dominica, Nov. 1... We are informed by Captain John COOK, master of the brigantine black prince, lately taken by the St. Peter American ship of 18 six pounders, 16 swivels and 150 men...

(322) Advertisements. Newbern, January 8. Whereas the Congress of Delegates for the United States of America have recommended it to the different States of the union, that loan offices should be established in each of them for the purpose of borrowing money to support the present war. And the general Assembly of the State of North-Carolina, having established one in the town of Newbern.. I hereby give notice that I am ready to receive into said office any sum or sums of money (not less than 200 dollars from any one individual)..on the receipt of which certificates will issue to the lenders for the amount, bearing an interest of six per cent. James GREEN Jun. Treasurer.

(323) Newbern, December 24. Hamilton BALLANTINE late of the island of Jamaica, attorney at law, acquaints the public that he purposes to reside in this State, where in the course of his practice he only wishes for such encouragement as his integrity to his clients and the justness of their cause merits..he purposes to attend the superior courts in the respective districts,...

(324) December 17. Strayed from camp near Halifax the 13th of October last two horses.. Any person that will give information of the said horses to the owner in camp in the 10th regiment, or my house in Dobbs County, shall be satisfactory rewarded. Matthias HARVY.

(325) State of North-Carolina, Dec. 27. To be sold to the highest bidder, at the next superior court in the town of Hillsborough, on the 27th day of March next, pursuant to a resolve of the general Assembly: The iron works on Deep-River in the County of Chatham..also a large quantity of land containing timber and stone sufficient to support said works, and an inexhaustible fund of excellent Iron Ore.

(325) (Cont.) The premises will be shewn any one desirous of seeing the same by Captain Balaam THOMSON living thereon..the Commissioners.

(326) Newbern, Jan. 9, 1771. All persons who have any demands against the estate of Thomas SPROTT A. B. deceased, are desired to make them known immediately... Joseph BLYTH, Administrator.

January 16, 1778. Number 411.

(327) In Congress, November 4, 1777. Resolved, That his Excellency Governor CASWELL, of North Carolina, be requested to erect a monument of the value of 500 dollars, at the expense of these United States, in honour of the memory of Brigadier General Francis NASH, who fell in the battle of Germantown on the 4th day of October, 1777, bravely contending for the independence of his country... Extract from the minutes, Charles THOMSON, Sec'ry.

(328) State of North-Carolina. By his Excellency Richard CASWELL, Esquire, Governor... A Proclamation. Whereas it appears by the petition of Captain John SHEPHERD, that sundry persons living near Occacock Bar, have unlawfully possessed themselves of a large quantity of goods, the property of said SHEPHERD, and part of the cargo of the snow Diamond, lately wrecked there..I do..issue this Proclamation, hereby offering a reward of 50 pounds to any white freeman who will, on oath, inform the Attorney General of this State, of the names and places of abode of all or any of the aforesaid persons. Given under my hand, and seal at arms, at Newbern, the 10th day of January, 1778, and in the second year of the independence of the said State. Richard CASWELL. By his Excellency's command. James GLASGOW Sec'ry.

(329) State of North Carolina. His Excellency Richard CASWELL, Esq; Governor... A Proclamation. Whereas it hath been certified to me, that the following persons have been appointed clerks of the superior courts of law within this state, to wit: John COOK, Esq; for the district of Newbern, George HOOPER, Esq; for the district of Wilmington, Henry GISSARD (or GIFFARD), Esq; for the district of Salisbury, Joseph TAYLOR, Esq; for the district of Hillsborough, Eaton HAYNES, Esq; for the district of Halifax, and Charles BONFIELD, Esq; for the district of Edenton; in consequence of which appointment..have appeared before me and qualified agreeable to law; I do..issue this proclamation notifiing to the good people of this State the qualifications..as clerks of the said courts respectively... Given under my hand..at Newbern, the 14th day of January 1778... Richard CASWELL. By his Excellency's command. James GLASGOW, Sec'ry.

(330) Advertisements. Springfield, Jan. 10. Five Dollars reward. Run away from the subscriber on Sunday night, the 28th instant, a negro woman named CAROLINA, the property of Robert CALF a minor, is supposed to be harboured by the negroes of Col. John PATTEN in Beaufort County. Whoever takes up and brings to me the said slave at Springfield four miles above Newbern, shall receive the..reward... Isaac PATRIDGE.

(331) Pitt County, Jan. 10. Ran away from the subscriber a negro man named YORK, about 21 years of age, well made, about 5 feet 9 inches

(331) (Cont.) high, with a pleasant countenance, and speaks broken
English..five dollars reward. Thomas GOUGH.

(332) Craven-County, Jan. 9, 1778. Whereas a final settlement on
the estate of Edward FRANCK deceased ought to be made at the next
court, It is therefore requested that all persons who have any demands
..bring them in immediately... Waightstill AVERY, Leah AVERY, Administrator, Administratrix, &c.

(333) Bath, January 10, 1778. To be rented immediately for one year
or longer..the large and commodious house where the subscriber now
lives..together with the plantation of near 3000 acres, 300 of which
are cleared..apply to Messrs. Thomas and Titus OGDEN, merchants in
Newbern, or to me at Bath. Also will be rented a plantation within
five miles of Bath, with a good clapboard house and dairy, containing
100 acres.. And on the 20th day of February next will be sold at vendue at Bath, near 100 head of cattle, 40 head of hogs, two plantation
horses, one mare, and some exceeding good household furniture..moho-
gony chairs, tables and looking glasses in set frames... William
PALMER.

January 23, 1778. Number 412.

(334) Baltimore, Dec. 23, 1777. Extract of a letter from East Bradford, Chester County, Dec. 12. "I this day went down to Haverford,
and there found the most destructive piece of work I ever saw. Your
brother Anthony MORRIS's house and place is robbed of every thing the
merciless wretches, the English, could take away: They have not even
left them or the children any thing of food, neither bed or blanket,
or any cloathing, except what they had on their backs. Everything of
his, yours, and your father's, they could not take off, they took
ca e to destroy; and what is worse, Anthony is wounded, but I hope
not mortally.. All the fingers of one hand are nearly cut off, and
the rest are so bad, that Dr. MORRIS was obliged to take one off; his
upper lip is split, a piece cut out of his nose, both cheeks cut;
after which they robbed him of his horse and money..he crept down to
one WEISS's, where he now lies; his wife is with him..FARR has taken
three of the children to his mother's.. I would be glad Mrs. MORRIS
would send me some linnen, &c. for them and the children; do send
them, for they have not any change of clothes till they receive them."

(335) Advertisements. Washington, Jan. 6, 1778. All persons who
have had dealings with SCOTT, IRWIN and COUPER, and where accounts remain unsettled, either at their Tarborough, Martinborough, or Washington stores, are requested to settle their accounts..for which purpose
one of the partners will attend at Beaufort and Pitt County courts,
and Henry Irwin TOOL, Esq; is empowered to settle..all..accounts with
their store at Tarborough. The Death of Col. Henry IRWIN, one of the
partners, makes it necessary that the accounts be immediately settled.
.. John COUPER.

(336) Newbern, Jan. 23, 1778. Monday last, the sloop Success Capt.
TUCKER from Bermuda..ran ashore on Cape Hatteras.. The Captain gives
this notice, that if the vessel, or any part of her rigging, sails,
or cargo, can be saved, he is willing to pay salvage for it. Apply to

(336) (Cont.) the Captain or Mr. John W. STANLEY Merchant in Newbern.

January 30, 1778. Number 413.

(337) Fish-Kill, December 18. The following two letters..between General PARSONS and General TRYON, shew the line of conduct the enemy mean to pursue. Maroneck, Nov. 21, 1777. Sir, Adding to the natural horrors of war, the most wanton destruction of property, is an act of cruelty unknown to civilized nations and unaccustomed in war, until the servants of the King of Great-Britain, have convinced the impartial world, no acts of inhumanity, no stretch of despotism, are too great to exercise towards those they term Rebels. Had any apparent advantage been derived from burning the houses on PHILIPS's Manor, last Monday, there would have been some reason to justify the measure; but when no benefit whatever can be proposed, by burning those buildings, and stripping the women and children of necessary apparel to cover them from the severity of a cold night, and captivating and leading in triumph to your line, in the most ignominious manner, the heads of those families; I know not what justifiable cause to assign for those acts of cruelty; nor can I conceive a necessity for your further order to destroy Tarry Town. It is not my inclination, sir, to war in this manner..necessity will oblige me to retaliate in kind upon your friends..unless your explicit disavowal of the conduct of your two Captains, EMMERICK and BA_NS, shall convince me, those houses were burned without your knowledge and against your order. I am, sir, your humble servant, Samuel H. PARSONS. (to) Gen. TRYON.

King's-Bridge Camp, November 23, 1777. Sir, Could I possibly conceive myself accountable to any revolted subject of the king of Great Britain, I might answer your letter, received by the flag of truce yesterday, respecting the conduct of the party under Capt. EMMERICK's command, upon the ___ _king of Peter and Cornelius VAN TASSEL. I have, however, candor enough to assure you..I should, were I in more authority, burn every Committee man's house within my reach, as I deem those agents the wicked instruments of the continued calamities of this country.. I am, Sir, your most obedient servant, William TRYON, Maj. Gen. (to) Gen. PARSONS.

This came out on Sunday the 23d inst. and by some means or other General DELANCEY's house, at Bloomindall, on York island, took fire the 25th night. Committee men, take care of your heads, the Alamance Heroe seems to be angry; we imagine General GATES and his Yankies give him rather more trouble than Harman HUSBANDS and the Regulators did.

(338) James DELANCEY, late sheriff of West-Chester, and Colonel of the enemy's militia, was taken last week by one of our scouts.. Last week a small party of men, made an excursion to Greenwich, about three miles from New-York..advanced to Oliver DELANCEY's..we hear five men were made prisoners, they set the house on fire, and hearing the alarm gun, in New-York, that it was time to decamp, crossed the river..and got safe off.

(339) New-London, December 19. .. A plan having been formed to bring off or destroy a magazine of military stores..the enemy had at Shetocket on Long-Island..on Tuesday night of last week part of two battalions of troops embarked from this state under convoy of the

(339) (Cont.) sloop Schuyler, and the Spy and Mifflin schooners..the
Faulkland, a British frigate..came across the Schuyler and two smaller
vessels, when the latter run ashore upon the island, but the former..
run on a spit of sand called the Old Man's, and was taken, with about
60 troops on board, among whom were the following officers, viz. Colonels FLY and WEBB, Capt. BUCKLAND, Lieut. RILEY, Ensign MUMFORD, Adjutant HOPKINS, and Quarter-master START, of WEBB's battalion, and
Ensigns NILES and ABBOT, and Adjutant WEST, of FLY's battalion. On
Thursday a party of men under Capt. HART, marched to Southold.. Col.
LIVINGSTON, who was taken at fort Montgomery, another Colonel, and a
Major..(who refused to give their paroles) have made their escape from
on board a prison ship at New York.

(340) New-York, November 20. Yesterday morning Mr. BRUSH, upwards
of 19 months a prisoner in Boston goal arrived here, from that place,
from whence he escaped on Wednesday evening the 5th instant.

(341) Boston, December 8. The following gentlemen are chosen by the
general Assembly of this State, as delegates to serve in the continental Congress the ensuing year, viz. Hon. John HANCOCK, Esq; Samuel
ADAMS, Esq; John ADAMS, Esq; Robert T. PAINE, Esq; Eldridge GERRY,
Esq; Francis DANA, Esq; and James LOVELL, Esq;.

(342) December 16. At the late meeting of this town it was voted,
that the thanks of the town be given to the Hon. John HANCOCK, Esq;
for his generous donation of 150 cords of wood to the poor of the
town in this time of distress.

(343) Capt. John LEECH is arrived at Salem with a prize brig...

(344) Newbern, January 30, 1778. A few days ago, died at her house
in Onslow County, much regretted, Mrs. WARBURTON; a Lady well known
to the Public, for the very elegant and genteel House of Entertainment
she has for many Years kept for the Accomodation of Travellers.

(345) Advertisements. Newbern, Jan. 20. To be hired for One Year.
Several fine young slaves... Mary GORDON.

(346) Newbern, Jan. 30. The purchasers at the sales of the prize
brig Hanover's cargo, who have not already paid, are requested to pay
off their accounts to the subscriber... Richard ELLIS, Agent.

February 6, 1778. Number 414.

(347) Burlington, December 24.. The legislature of New-Jersey, at
their last sitting at Prince-town, appointed the Hon. John WITHERSPOON,
Abraham CLARK, Jonathan ELMER, Nathaniel SCUDDER, and Elias BOUDINOT,
Esquires, delegates to represent this state in Congress.

(348) Baltimore, Dec. 30, 1777... January 13. Last Friday Capt.
William NUTEN, in the sloop Pennsylvania-Farmer, arrived here in 25
days from Curacoa...

(349) State of North-Carolina. By his Excellency Richard CASWELL,
Esq; Governor.. A Proclamation. Whereas it will be difficult if not

(349) (Cont.) impracticable to supply the army of the United States
of America with beef, pork, bacon and salt, unless the exportation and
transportation thereof be prohibited; I..issue this Proclamation hereby prohibiting the exportation of beef, pork, bacon and common salt
from this State after this date, until the expiration of Thirty Days,
except such as shall be sent thereout for the support of the continental army.. Given under my hand,..at Newington (sic), the first day
of February, Anno domini 1778.. Richard CASWELL. By his Excellency's
command. J. GLASGOW, Sec'ry.

February 13, 1778. Number 415.

(350) Williamsburg, Jan. 30. Extract of a letter from Edenton, dated
Jan. 22. "Letters from Bourdeaux, of the 6th of December last, _en-
tion, that Dr. FRANKLIN had been stabbed, but it was tho't _uld get
over it. The king's speech is come over, and it seems __ is determined to push on the war."

(351) Newbern, Feb. 13, 1778. On Wednesday last, died at his house
in this town, after a very tedious and afflicting indisposition, David
BARRON, Esq; a gentleman who, in the course of a few years, with great
industry and assiduity, has acquired a handsome fortune, with a fair
and unblemished character.

(352) Advertisements. Newbern, Feb. 11. The subscriber takes this
method to acquaint the public in general and his friends in particular
that he has declined keeping tavern but still continues entertaining
any gentlemen and ladies travelling through this State..at his house
as private lodgings... Edmond WRENFORD.

February 20, 1778. Number 416.

(353) York-Town, Jan. 3. The following elegiac lines were occasioned
by the death of the Hon. Brigadier General Francis NASH, of North-
Carolina, who died of his wounds, the 7th of October last, which he
received on the morning of the 4th, as he was gallantly leading on
his brigade to charge the enemy near Germantown...

(354) Charlestown, Jan. 29. The Speech of his Excellency John RUT-
LEDGE, Esq; president and commander in chief in and over the state of
South Carolina, to the legislative council and general assembly met
at Charlestown, on Friday Jan. 9th, 1778...

(355) To his Excellency John RUTLEDGE, Esquire, president..of the
state of South Carolina: The Address of the Legislative Council of
the said State. May it please your Excellency,... In the legislative
council the 14th day of Jan. 1778. By order of the house; Hugh RUT-
LEDGE, Speaker.

(356) To his Excellency John RUTLEDGE, Esquire, president..of the
state of South Carolina; The Address of the General Assembly... By
order of the house, Thomas BEE, Speaker. Jan. 14.

(357) Charlestown, Jan. 29. On Thursday the 15th instant, a little
after 4 o'clock in the morning, a fire was discovered in the bake-

(357) (Cont.) house of one MOORE, at the north end of union street..
The fire was so rapid in its progress, that before 12 o'clock it had
entirely destroyed all Union street; the south side of Queen street
from Mrs. DOYLEY's house to the bay-greatest part of Chalmers's alley-
all the bay, excepting 15 houses, from Queen street to Granville's
Bastion-the north side of broad street from Mr. Thomas SMITH's house
to the bay; the south side of the same from Mr. SARRAZIN's to Mr.
GUERARD's house-all Gadsden's alley-Elliott street excepting two houses
-Bedon's alley-the east side of Church street from broad street to
Stoll's alley, excepting 5 tenements-and the whole of Tradd street to
the eastward of Church street.. Much praise is due to the officers
and soldiers quartered in town, who afforded every assistance in their
power to the inhabitants..Capt. BIDDLE with a party of his crew, also
assisted.. The number of dwelling houses destroyed..is upward of 250
..a number of lives lost, six, some of whom were negroes.

(358) Advertisements. State of North Carolina, Craven County, ss.
By James DAVIS and John FONVILLE, Esqrs. two of the Justices for the
said county. Complaint hath been made to us, by Ann BARRON, that a
mulatto man named LEWIS, 5 feet 6 inches high, well set, has black
hair which curles naturally, remarkable large black eyes and thick
lips, his face is freckled, late the property of Major David BARRON,
deceased, is ran away..and is supposed to have gone to Virginia. These
are therefore to command the said slave forthwith to surrender himself
.: And we do..declare, if the said slave doth not surrender himself,
and return home, immediately..that then any person may kill or destroy
the said slave..without accusation or impeachment of any crime or of-
fence..or any penalty.: James DAVIS, J. FONVILLE. N. B. Whoever
apprehends the said slave, and secures him in Newbern gaol, shall have
50 dollars reward, and handsomely rewarded if secured in any other
gaol in this state. Ann BARRON.

(359) Newbern, Feb. 18. Notice is hereby given to the freeholders
and freemen of the county of Craven, that an election will be held at
the courthouse in Newbern, on the 10th and 11th days of March next,
for electing one senator, and two members of the house of commons, to
'epresent the said county in general assembly, and..inhabitants of the
town of Newbern are hereby noticed to attend and elect one member to
represent the said town. J. BRYAN, shff.

(360) The printers in the state of North-Carolina, are requested to
publish in their newspapers, the following advertisement: At a general court martial held at white marsh, in the state of Pennsylvania,
on the 2d day of December 1777, by order of his Excellency General
WASHINGTON. Capt. VAIL of the second North-Carolina battalion, charged
with Cowardice, at the battle of Germantown, was tried, found guilty
of that crime, and sentenced therefor to be cashiered; and to have his
crime, name, place of abode, and punishment published in the newspapers
in and about the camp, and of that particular state from which he came;
and that it should be deemed scandalous for any officer to associate
with him... T. PICKERING, A. G.

March 6, 1778. Number 418.

(361) London. Extract of a letter from Mr. Manduit DUPLESIS, now a

(361) (Cont.) French officer in the service of the United States, written to his brother in Porte L'Orient, dated April 19, 1777.."After having travelled through New-England..we came to the grand army on the second of April, commanded by General WASHINGTON,..; his looks, manner of speaking, and conduct to every body, bespeaks the finished gentleman; but his assiduous labours, and great penetration, declare the compleat General. He is beloved by his troops, (39 thousand regulars) accessible to every body, and determines causes in the army with justice and wisdom; he protects the officers from insult, and the common soldiers from ill usage..."

(362) Advertisements. Newbern, Feb. 24, The subscriber has for sale a quantity of medecines which are just imported,..Rheubarb, Jesuits bark, glauber and epsom salts, tartar emetic, jallap, ipecacnanna, camphor, mercurious dulcis, corrosive sublimate, cantharides, sal nitre, sulphur, crem of tartar, crude salarmoniac, myrrh, cinnamon, cloves, mace, &c. William PASTEUR.

(363) Newbern, Feb. 21. To the Freeholders in Craven County. Gentlemen, Public business requires my attendance at Fredericksburg, in Virginia, at the time of our annual election; I therefore..apologise for my absence, return you thanks for your former confidence, and again offer myself a candidate to represent you in the next general Assembly. James COOR.

(364) Newbern, Jan. 28. Lost on Sunday the 25th of this instant, a gold watch, the case engraved with the maker's name (John Bt. lenoir, Paris) upon the face.. Any person having found it will be handsomely rewarded on bringing it to Mr. OGDEN...

(365) Newbern, Feb. 22. Whereas the subscriber gave his note of hand for a sum of money payable to Mr. William EWEN on order, the 20th of January last, with lawful interest from the date, and as I have proferred payment..with interest..to the said Mr. EWEN..who refused delivering it; saying he had it not in his possession; I therefore publish this as my intention of not paying any interest to any person ..after the time of proferring payment..as aforesaid.. Daniel BARRY.

(366) Gasper BEAUFORT, from Philadelphia, gives this public notice, that on Monday next he proposes opening a school in this town, at the house of Widow WO FLEY, to teach the French tongue; to read, right, and speak it gramatically.. His price will be 30 shillings per month.

March 13, 1778. Number 419.

(367) Advertisements. Craven-County, Feb. 25, 1778. Mr. DAVIS, please to insert the following notification in your paper for one month. Whereas I did on the 14th day of July 1774, execute two bonds, one for the payment of L300 and the other..of L400 proclamation money, to the then honou able Samuel CORNELL Esq; in which bonds Messrs. Jacob BLOUNT, Farnifold GREEN, and Hardy BRYAN, were bound as my securities, and as the time of payment mentioned in said bonds are long since expired, and they remain still undischarged owing to Mr. CORNELL's absence from this state, ..I now give..notice to the agents, attorneys or assignes of Mr. CORNELL..that I am ready to discharge the

(367) (Cont.) above mentioned bonds... William BRYAN.

(368) Newbern, North-Carolina, Feb. 26. Run away from the subscriber a mulatto man named ABRAHAM, who he lately bought from Mr. Isaac PAT- RIDGE of this place,..near..6 feet high, tolerable good house carpen- ter and shoemaker, about 40 years of age..will appear well dressed.. and has a considerable sum of money with him, he was seen about 10 days since on his way to Holly Shelter, in company with a mulatto man named LEWIS, belonging to Mrs. BARRON, of this town, both on horseback he was the property of the late Major David BARRON, deceased, he is 18 years of age, and about 5 feet 6 inches high, well set, has black hair which curles naturally, remarkable large eyes, his face is much freckled, he will also appear well dressed, as he has a plenty of clothes and money..they will..keep together..change their names, and endeavour to pass as freemen..make..their way for South Carolina, to enter on board some vessel..to..escape to the West Indies, as ABRAHAM has relations in St. Eustatia..100 dollars reward, if taken out of the state 200 dollars... Wilson BLOUNT.

(369) Newbern, March 11. As Mr. BEAUFORT has attended at the house ..in his former advertisement, and has not met with such encourage- ment as he deserves, in teaching the French, he intends to continue one month and no longer...

(370) Advertisements. Newbern, March 20. Our good customers are desired to take notice, that the third day of April next completes a year of the publication of this gazette since it was last resumed...

(371) A List of Letters remaining in the Post-Office, Newbern, viz. Mr. Stephen STIMSON, 1 letter, received 6th April last. Mr. James FEREBEE, 1 do., 11th May. Mr. John ETHEREDGE, 1 do. 9th June. Col. William DAVIS, 1 do., 16th June. Mr. John HOUSE, 1 do., 7th July. Capt. Thomas KILL, 1 do., 1st Sept.. Capt. Francis HODGSON, 1 do., 8th Sept. Miss Cornelia LENT, 1 do., 9th Sept. Joseph HADY, 1 do., 29th Sept. Gilbert GRAY, near Mr. ORMES, Trent, 1 do., 5 th Oct. Mr. John POWELL, Edgcomb County, 1 do., 22d Nov. Mr. George SAGG, Pitt County, 1 do., 13th Dec. John TURNER, Esq; 1 do., 21st Dec. Messrs. CUNNINGHAM and Co., 1 do., 17th Jan. Job THARP, near New-River, 1 do., 21st Feb. Mr. Richard LEEVIUS, 1 do., 28th Feb. Mr. John SPICER, 1 do., 1st March. Richard COGDELL, D. P. M.

(372) Georgetown, S. C. Feb. 8. Run away from the subscriber on Saturday night last, a negro man named JACK, 5 feet 10 inches high, 25 years of age, very black,..is very artful and speaks good English being born in Virginia, and am of opinion he is gone to North Carolina, to a place called Woodstock at Pungo..reward of 20 pounds currency..; Epaphras NOTT.

(373) State of North-Carolina, Craven County, ss. By James DAVIS and Richard ELLIS, Esqrs. two of the justices for the said County. Where- as complaint hath been made to us, by Ann GRAVES, that a negro fellow named QUASH, 5 feet 6 inches high, slim made, and very black, is ran away. These are therefore to command the said slave forthwith to sur- render himself, and return home to his said Mistress... And we do hereby..declare if the said slave doth not surrender himself, and re-

(373) (Cont.) turn home..any person may kill or destroy the said
slave..without accusation..of any crime..or penalty... James DAVIS,
Richard ELLIS. N. B. Whoever apprehends the said slave, and secures
him in Newbern gaol, shall have 10 dollars, and 10 pounds for his
head. Ann GRAVES.

April 3, 1778. Number 422.

(374) Advertisements. All persons are forewarned from cutting wood,
or committing any trespass on the lands of the subscriber near Newbern, as she is determined to make an example of the first person
found guilty thereof. Deborah SMITH.

(375) Newbern, April 3. Ten Dollars Reward. Run away from this
place a negro fellow named SALEM, about 5 feet 9 inches high, lusty
and well made, speaks good English... Frances BATCHELOR.

(376) Edenton, March 25. To be sold at public vendue, on Tuesday
the 5th of May next,.. The dwelling house, kitchen, store-house..
situate in the town of Edenton, whereon the late Mrs. Elizabeth WAL-
LACE lived..on one lot of land.. The dwelling house consists of four
rooms below, three of which have fireplaces, and six good bed chambers
above, wherein are two fireplaces.. Also a dwelling house and kitchen
with five good lots, now occupied by Mr. SINCLAIR in the said town...

(377) Rocky-Point, New-Hanover County, Feb. 23. To be sold, two valuable tracts of land, containing 1280 acres, situate in Cumberland
County on each side of the N. W. branch of Cape Fear river, beginning
a quarter of a mile above the mouth of Rockfish creek.. These lands
were patented by John Baptista ASHE, Esq; deceased, the 6th May 1730..
Thomas MOSELEY.

April 10, 1778. Number 423.

(378) State of North Carolina. By his Excellency Richard CASWELL,
Esq; Governor.. A Proclamation.. And whereas the honourable the
American Congress, hath resolved "that it be recommended to the united
states of America, to set apart Wednesday the 22d day of April..to be
observed as a day of Fasting, Humiliation, and Prayer, that at one
time, and with one voice, the inhabitants may acknowledge the righ-
teous dispensations of Divine Providence.." I have therefore..issued
this proclamation hereby requiring the inhabitants of this state, to
pay proper regard to the said resolution of Congress.. Given under
my hand..the 7th day of April,..1778. Richard CASWELL. By his Excellency's command, J. GLASGOW, Secretary.

(379) Advertisements. Newbern, April 10. All persons having demands
against the estate of Richard STELE, deceased, are requested to bring
in their accounts.. I intend in a few days, to make a final settlement of my accounts. Edward Boucher HODGES.

(380) Broad-Creek, on Neuse River, April 9. On Saturday night, April
the 4th, broke into the house of the subscriber at the head of Green's
Creek, where I had some small property under the care of Ann DRIGGUS,
a free negro woman, two men in disguise, who with marks on their faces

(380) (Cont.) and clubs in their hands, beat and wounded her terribly
and carried away four of her children, three girls and a boy, the big-
gest of said girls got off in the dark and made her escape, one of the
girl's name is BECCA, and other CHARITA, the boy is named SHADRACK;
she says the men were William MUNDAY and Charles TOWZER, a sailor
lately from Newbern, these men were on board of a boat belonging to
Kelly CASON, and was with him in the boat about the middle of the day.
Fifty dollars reward will be given to any person who will stop the
children and apprehend the robbers... John CARUTHERS.

(381) Buckskin Stands at my plantation in Pitt-County this season...
Edward SALTER.

(382) Newbern, April 3. Notice is hereby given to the freemen of the
county of Craven, that there will be an election held at the court-
house in Newbern on Easter monday the 20th of this instant, for electing seven proper persons to serve as overseers of the poor. John
BRYAN.

April 24, 1778. Number 425.

May 1, 1778. Number 426.

(383) Extract from General Orders. Camp, Valley-Forge, March 27,
1778. ..The commander in chief hopes these considerations will in-
fluence officers in the ensuing campaign, to provide themselves with
those necessaries only, which cannot be dispensed with, and with the
means of carrying them in the most easy and convenient manner..to em-
ploy as few waggons as possible, and to make use of pack horses, as
far as may be practicable... Alexander SCAMMELL, Adj. Gen.

(384) Baltimore, April 7. Major General GREEN, we hear, is appointed
quarter-master general in the room of Major General MIFFLIN, who is
now one of the Hon. Board of war.

(385) The Hon. John ADAMS, Esq; is now on his passage to France, having been despatched on a special embassy to that court from the united
states.

(386) Williamsburg, April 17. The St. Taminy, Capt. CUNINGHAM, in
12 days from St. Eustatia, is just arrived in James river with a very
valuable cargo. In her came passenger Mr. Thomas SHORE, of Petersburg.

(387) Newbern, May 1. Since our last, the General Assembly now sitting here, proceeded to the appointment of continental delegates, when
the choice fell on Cornelius HARNETT, and John PENN, Esqrs. and the
Hon. John WILLIAMS, Esq; speaker of the house of commons; which office
vacating his seat in that house, the Hon. Thomas BENBURY, Esq; was unanimously elected to the chair in his room, and seated accordingly.

(388) Advertisements. Dobbs, April 20, 1778. Run away from the Subscriber..a new negro fellow..name of PETER, about 5 feet 5 inches high,
about 40 years of age..5 l. reward   Benjamin CASWELL.

(389) Run away from the subscriber in Bladen county, a negro man

(389) (Cont.) named CAESAR, about 5 feet 5 or 6 inches high, about 20 years of age.. A reward of 10 1...to any person who shall apprehend and confine him in any gaol..or shall execute him according to law, he being outlawed the 14th of April 1778. Thomas AMIS.

(390) For sale, at the next superior court to be held for the district of Newbern, a tract of land situate on Trent, in Craven county, known by the name of the Tuckahoe meadows. For terms apply..at Newbern. Jas. IREDELL.

(391) Newbern, April 24. This is to inform Usebious STONE that a tract of land and stock of cattle, was left to him by Marmaduke NORFLEET, deceased, late of Northampton County, and that on his making application to the subscribers or either of them, he may receive the same. Reuben NORFLEET, W. BAKER, J. HOGUN.

(392) Newbern, April 24. Made his escape from the deputy sheriff of Craven County, on the 20th instant, William ALCOCK, who was taken on a writ at the suit of Edward Boucher HODGES. Whoever apprehends and delivers him to me shall have twenty shillings reward. John KENNEDY.

(393) Halifax, March 14. Ten Dollars Reward. Deserted from me the 12th instant on their march for Halifax, two soldiers belonging to the 5th battalion of this state, William WATSON and Charles PETERS; WATSON has deserted five times..also cost the public 20 odd pounds for taking him up and jail fees, he is about 5 feet 10 inches high, dark complected, black hair, lives on or near Bay river, below Newbern. PETERS is a East-India Indian, formerly the property of Mr. THOMLINSON in Newbern. Whoever delivers one or both of the above deserters to me at Bath or to any continental officer, taking their receipt for the same, shall have the above reward. Ben. STEADMAN.

(394) Craven County, April 17. Taken up by the subscriber, near musseleshell, a large mare... Elisha STAFFORD.

May 8, 1778. Number 427.

(395) Yorktown. The following is taken from a Philadelphia newspaper, of the 17th of April, published by James ROBERTSON...

(396) Deserted from Col. CHARIOLL's regiment, in the service of this state, a soldier named Marc CLEMENT, a native of France, about 5 feet 5 inches high, dark complection..speaks bad English..five pounds reward.

(397) Run away from the subscriber at Wilmington in June 1776, a negroe fellow named PRINCE, 5 feet 6 inches high, 20 years of age, slim bodied and large legs, wants one or more of his fore teeth, marked with the smallpox and whip. Forty dollars to any person that will secure said negro so that I may get him. Robert ROWAN. Campbelton, May 1.

(398) I Gave a bond to Mr. John KINCHEN of Hillsborough in 1775, payable in January 1778, which said bond the said KINCHEN endorsed to Mr. MC NAIR, the 1st of March in Hillsborough; this is to desire Mr. MC

(398) (Cont.) NAIR, or his agents to produce the said bond to me, as
I am ready to discharge it, and will not after this pay any interest
on the said bond. Also a note to John CRUDEN,..payable in 1776..pro-
duce said note, as I am now ready to discharge the same... Roger
MOORE. Cape Fear, May 1.

(399) To Be Sold a small schooner, 35 tons burthen, now lying at Newbern..was a privateer in the present war... William GOOD.

(400) Taken up by the subscriber a negro fellow who says his name
formerly was TOM, but now he says his name is SCIPIO.. The owner is
desired to prove him his property, pay charges, and take him away.
John BURRUSS. Wilmington, April 29.

May 15, 1778. Number 428.

(401) London, Jan. 5. .. Dec. 25. In consequence of the advertisement for the relief of the American prisoners, a most respectable
meeting was yesterday held at the King's arms tavern, Cornhill. In
proof of their extreme wretchedness, the following petition from the
prisoners, addressed to a noble lord, and several letters..were read:
May it please your Lordship, We the subscribers, natives of America,
being at this time prisoners of war, and closely confined in his majesty's prison at Portsmouth.. In number we are (at Portsmouth) about
140, all of us in want of warm cloathing, and many are actually without a shoe or stocking to their feet. And to add to those hardships..
an overseer..who seems..totally void of humanity. He detains every..
supply sent to us..or sells it.. We are not allowed candle or fire
in this extreme season, which must prove fatal to many in a cold and
exposed prison... Given under our hands in the prison in Portsmouth,
the 1st of December, 1777. Herman COUTER, commander of the Oliver.
Byrd CHAMBERLAYNE, 1st lieutenant of the Muschetto. George CHAMBER-
LAYNE, 2d lieutenant ditto. John M'NICKAL, surgeon ditto. Robert
M'CAVE, prizemaster, belonging to Capt. WEEKS. William WILLIAMS,
master of the brig general Montgomery. John COCHRAN, boatswain of
the Yankee; in prison 18 months. Joseph SMITH, Thomas CLARK, James
GIDOONWORK, James MOTTY, sailors.

(402), Newbern, May 15. Extract of a letter from his Excellency Henry
LAURENS, president of Congress, to his Excellency Richard CASWELL, Esq;
dated York town, April 24...

(403) Advertisements. Run away from the subscriber..Isaac BELL, an
apprentice boy, about 17 years of age, 4 feet 6 inches high, light
hair, a remarkable flat face,..I imagine he has gone down to Mr. Philip NEALE's plantation, on Neuse river. Whoever brings said apprentice
to me, shall have 10 dollars... James ARANKS. Newbern, May 13.

(404) The subscriber has for sale at the town of Beaufort, Carteret
county, a new vessel..55 feet keel strait rabbet, 11 feet rake forward, 18 and a half feet beam, and 7 feet and a half hold. Abiel
CHENEY.

(405) For sale by private contract, the good sloop called the Caswell,
burthen 90 tons..lying at Bogue inlet..with the..cargo on board...

(405) (Cont.) Any person inclining to treat for the said sloop and cargo..apply to Monsieur DIVIVIER, at Mr. Wm. HEATH's, or to Mr. Thomas OGDEN, merchant in Newbern... Newbern, May 15.

May 22, 1778. Number 429.

(406) Annapolis, May 5, 1778. Extract of a letter from his Excellency the President of Congress, to Mr. William LUX, of Baltimore. York-Town, May 3. Sir,..You will be soon fully informed of the treaties of alliance and commerce between the court of Versailles and the united states of America; A copy of a letter, which I here inclose, will in the mean time, give the great outlines. Copy of a letter from the Hon. Benjamin FRANKLIN, Silas DEANE, and Arthur LEE, Esquires. Pasey, near Paris, Feb. 8, 1778. Honorable Sir,...

(407) Advertisements. I Have just opened a large assortment of fresh imported medicines..would be glad to supply others, at the lowest terms..of Peruvian bark, camphire, sweet mercury, opium, rheubarb, jailap, Ipecacuanha, aloes, myrrh, gummastick, magnesia, Spanish flies Venice treacle, borax, saltpetre, volatile salt of hartshorn, do. of salamoniac, camamile flower, brimstone, and flowers of sulphur, &c. Alex. GASTON. Newbern, May 22.

(408) To be sold, at the white rock, near Newbern, a small quantity of Indian corn, black ey'd pease, pork, bacon, and hog's fat. for terms apply to W. AVERY.

May 29, 1778. Number 430.

(409) Yorktown, May 13. From a Philadelphia paper, of May 9, 1778, printed by James HUMPHREYS junior,...

(410) Newbern, May 29. Just opened and to be sold, at Thomas SIT-GREAVES and Son's shop.. A Large and general assortment of goods...

June 6, 1778. Number 431.

(411) To the Honourable James IREDELL, Esq; one of the Judges of the Superior Court held at Edenton, for the district of Edenton, on the first Day of May 1778. We, the Grand Jury for the district of Edenton, return you our thanks for the Charge which you was pleased to deliver to us at the opening of this court...

(412) Advertisements. To be sold, by the subscriber at his store, at Col. COGDELL's, superfine Virginia flour, and butter in kegs and firkins... Lory BROTHERS.

(413) To be hired out by the Year or Month, several house servants.. appply to Mary GORDON. Newbern, June 6.

(414) To be preremptorily sold, at private sale, on or after, and not before, the 10th of July next: The valuable and well known two saw-mills and grist-mill, in Dunant or Black-creek, in Carteret-county, with about 2000 acres of land adjoining to, and round the extensive pond... A full tide flows up to the tail of the mills, 15 miles by

69

(414) (Cont.) water from..Beaufort, on Core-Sound, about five miles
in a direct line from the sea, and not further the shortest and passa-
ble way to HOWARD's mill, on Neuse River.. The terms may be known,
and a plan of the settlement seen,..by applying to John WILLIAMS in
Newbern.. The reason the owner is determined to sell is, that he is
not in circumstances to pursue his plan to perfection, and too far
advanced in years to bear the fatigue much longer. Robert WILLIAMS.

June 13, 1778. Number 432.

(415) A Address of the Congress to the Inhabitants of the United
States of America. Friends and Countrymen,... By order of Congress,
Henry LAURENS, President. In Congress, May 9, 1778. Resolved, that
it be recommended to ministers of the Gospel, of all denominations,
to read, or cause to be read, immediately after divine service, the
above address..in their respective churches and chapels... Published
by order of Congress. Charles THOMSON, Sec.

(416) Advertisements. To be sold at public vendue, on Saturday the
27th instant, at Newbern: One half of the Brigantine Betsey, part of
the estate of Major David BARRON, deceased...

June 20, 1778. (Fragment)

(417) Newbern, June 20. Last week, Mr. Thomas OGDEN, of this town,
was married to Miss Phebe STARKEY, eldest daughter of John STARKEY,
Esq; of Onslow County; a most engageing and agreeable young lady,
amply possessed of beauty, merit and fortune.

(418) Advertisements. Strayed or stolen from the subscriber..a black
horse..Twenty dollars reward will be given to any person that will
bring him to the subscriber in Dobbs county, near the Old Ford, or
Mr. John WRIGHT in Duplin County. Peter DIGGINS. June 19.

(419) Notice is hereby given, that, agreeable to an act of assembly
passed last session a court house for the county of Orange, is to be
built in the town of Hillsborough; and the commissioners having determined to build the same with brick, any person willing to undertake
the same, will be treated with by applying to Nath ROCHESTER, William
COURTNEY, Com. Hillsborough, June 13.

June 26, 1778. Number 434.

(420) Boston, April 28...May 7. Friday last arrived at Portsmouth
the continental frigate Deane, Samuel NICHOLSON, Esq; commander, in
63 days from France...

(421) Advertisements. Urbanna, Virginia, Middlesex county, April 27.
If Joseph WHITLY of Orange county, North Carolina, and nephew of Thomas WHITLY, late of Middlesex-county, deceased, will apply to the subscriber, he will hear of something to his advantage. James ROSS.

(422) To be sold for ready money, two likely young negro fellows..
and a house wench..apply to either..John GREEN. John COOK.

July 3, 1778. Number 435.

(423) Baltimore, June 6. Extract of a letter from camp, dated May 27. At Germantown I was overtaken by Mr. COOMB the elder, who has thoughtproper to take the oath prescribed, and claim benefit of the law.. Philadelphia was certainly to be evacuated by the enemy. This unexpected revolution of government..has thrown the loyalists into the utmost horror and despair. Mr. GALLOWAY, Mr. SHOEMAKER, Mr. POTTS, and Mr. Dan. COX, are to go with the enemy. Mr. John LAWRENCE, Andrev ALLEN, Enoch STORY, Mr. AIRY and..other citizens also go with them. The following gentlemen have resolved not to leave the city. Mr. Tench COX, Dr. William SMITH, Mr. STRINGER, Mr. COOMB jun. and James ALLEN. .. Thomas LIVESLY is to be out today, to deliver himself up.. General HOWE embarked last Sunday at noon. Before he left the city, Israel PEMBERTON, it is said, waited on him for payment of damages done to his property to the amount of several thousand pounds.. Whig and tory have suffered indiscriminate ruin in and near the city.. Mr. Samuel BURGE is so affected by his loss as to be thought out of his reason.

(424) Advertisements. To the Public. The United States Loan Office at Newbern, still remains open... James GREEN jun. Treasurer. Loan Office, North Carolina, June 30.

(425) To be sold, the well known farm whereon I now live, adjacent to the lands of Brig. Gen. John ASHE, containing 1030 acres, 280 of which is arable, situate on the sound in New-Hanover county, 20 miles from Wilmington, and nearly opposite a fine bold inlet... New-Hanover County June 15. Bishop DUDLEY.

July 10, 1778. Number 436.

(426) Advertisements. To be sold on Monday the 13th instant, by the subscribers at their store, Colonel COGDELL's house, sundry dry goods ... Lory BROTHERS.

(427) All persons indebted to David BARRON and Co. and David BARRON, deceased..are desiredto make payment..any demands against the said estate..make them known to Edward BRYAN, who is empowered, will attend at the store of the late Mr. BARRON... Newbern, June 10. By the Executors.

(428) The subscribers to Messrs. DIXON and HUNTER's gazette in New-bern, and in the counties of Craven, Dobbs, and Onslow, are hereby de-sired to take notice, that every subscriber's account is made out to the 31st of December next... The subscribers to Mr. Alexander PURDEE for his gazette, will take notice, that the year for which they last paid is expired in May and June last... Richard COGDELL. Newbern, June 30.

July 17, 1778. Number 437.

(429) In Congress, June 17, 1778. Whereas many letters, addressed to individuals of these United Stated, have been lately received from England through the conveyance of the enemy; and some of them, which

(429) (Cont.) have been under the inspection of members of Congress,
are found to contain ideas insidiously calculated to divide and de-
lude the good people of these states; Resolved, That it be and it is
hereby earnestly recommended to the legislative and executive author-
ities of the several states, to..take the most effectual measures to
put a stop to so dangerous and criminal a correspondence. Resolved,
That the commander in chief, and the commanders in each and every military department be, and he and they are hereby directed to carry the
measures recommended in the above resolution into the most effectual
execution. Extract from the minutes, Charles THOMSON, Sec.

(430) Advertisements. State of North Carolina, Craven County, ss.
By Alexander GASTON and Richard ELLIS, Esquires, two of the Justices
for the said County. Whereas complaint hath been made to us by Frederick FONVILLE, that a negro slave named PETER, black fellow, aged
about 44 years, about 5 feet 5 inches high, ran away in December last.
These are therefore to command the said slave forthwith to surrender
himself, and return home to his said Master..if the said slave doth
not surrender himself..immediately after the publication of these presents, that then any person may kill or destroy the said slave..with-
out accusation or impeachment of any crime... Alex. GASTON. Richard
ELLIS. N. B. Whoever apprehends the said slave, and delivers him to
me, shall have 10 dollars, or 20 dollars for his head. Frederick
FONVILLE.

(431) Run away from the subscriber a new-negro fellow named BEN, a-
bout five feet eight inches high, between 30 and 40 years of age,
speaks bad English, marked on each arm with his country marks.. Whoever informs Robert CAKE, in Martin county, of said negro, so that he
may be found, shall receive ₤10 reward. Robert HARGRAVE, June 20.

July 24, 1778. Number 438.

(432) Williamsburg, July 10. We hear from the eastern shore, that
on the 29th ult. two privateers, of 10 and 12 guns, took a brig at the
mouth of Sinepuxent loaded with tobacco, belonging to Blair M'CLANAG-
HAN, merchant in Philadelphia.

(433) Newbern, July 18, 1778. On the morning of the first instant,
a small schooner arrived at Edenton, mounting two 3 pounders and two
swivels, with six English and four French sailors on board, she formerly belonged to one ETHERIDGE of Currituck, and some time past was
cut out of Old Currituck inlet, by John MC LEAN and Samuel DONALDSON,
and retaken by the inhabitants of Currituck...

(434) July 24, 1778. Yesterday several gentlemen arrived here from
Edenton by whom..we have the following important advices, viz. That
a French fleet of 14 sail of the line and four frigates are actually
arrived from France..arrived at Sandy Hook, and compleatly blocked up
New-York. We have no certain intelligence from the army since the
battle, only that General LEE is under an arrest for disobeying orders.
..and that General CADWALLADER and General CONWAY have had a duel, in
which General CONWAY was killed.

(435) Advertisements. Mr. Joseph BLYTH has opened school in the pub-

(435) (Cont.) lic school-house. And will teach Latin, English, Arithmetic, Geography, Geometry, Trigonometry, and several other of the most useful branch of the Mathematics... Newbern, July 24.

(436) One Hundred And Fifty Dollars Reward. Stolen from on board the ship Cornell, One Thousand Dollars, most of it in thirty dollar bills... C. BIDDLE. Newbern, July 16.

(437) This is to inform the public, that Geo. HARRISON intends opening a school on Monday next, opposite Mrs. DEWEY, where gentlemen and ladies may depend upon having their children carefully instructed in the English language, writing and cyphering. Also the French language taught. Newbern, July 24.

(438) Stolen from the subscriber on the 15th of July, a middle sized dark-bay horse.. Whoever will deliver the horse and the thief to me, in Craven county, near Newbern, shall have 20 dollars, or the horse alone 10 dollars... Joseph COART.

(439) On Thursday the 6th of August, will be sold to the highest bidder for ready money: The ship Harmony-Hall just arrived from Old France.. J. W. STANLY, T. & T. OGDEN, Newbern, July 24.

(440) Rich-Lands, New-River, July 23. Whereas Mr. Lewis WILLIAMS gave a note of hand payable to Mr. John OWENS, merchant in Newbern, for the sum of 35 pounds, and as I have, as attorney for Lewis WILLIAMS, applyed for, and cannot find who has the note, I request Mr. OWENS, or his attorney, to produce the note, as I am ready to discharge it, and will not after this date, pay interest on it. Nath. B. WILLIAMS.

July 31, 1778. Number 439.

(441) Philadelphia, July 4, 1778. Paris, May 18, 1778. Gentlemen, Certain intelligence having been received, that 11 British ships of war..are in the road of St. Hellens, near Portsmouth, bound for North America, and the United States being in alliance with France, you are requested, as speedily as possible, to convey this information to the commanders of any French fleet, or ships of war in America, by sending them this letter, and also to publish the contents of it in all the continental newspapers... B. FRANKLIN. John ADAMS. To the Governor, or any Counsellor, or Senator, or member of any house of Representatives, in any of the Thirteen United States of America. Read in Congress, July 8, 1778... Charles THOMSON, Sec.

(442) In Congress, July 7, 1778. Resolved Unanimously, that the thanks of Congress be given to General WASHINGTON for the activity with which he marched from the camp at Valley Forge in pursuit of the enemy, for his distinguished exertions in forming the order of battle, and for his great good conduct in leading on the attack and gaining the important victory of Monmouth, over the British grand army under the immediate command of Lieut. Gen. Sir Henry CLINTON, in their march from Philadelphia to New-York. Resolved, that General WASHINGTON be directed to signify the thanks of Congress to the gallant officers and men under his command...

(443) Baltimore, July 7. Capt. FAUNTLEROY, of Virginia, was slain in the battle of Monmouth.

(444) Newbern, July 31, 1778. Extract of a letter from John PENN Esq; delegate at Congress, to his Excellency the Governor, dated Philadelphia, July 15, 1778...

(445) Since our last died, Mr. John CLITHERAL, a very ancient and worthy inhabitant of this town; many years in the commission of the peace; a quiet and inoffensive neighbour, and a pious and good christian.

(446) Advertisements. Ten Dollar Reward. Stolen on Monday night last, a man's saddle newly covered... Isaac PATRIDGE. Spring Field, July 29.

(447) Deserted from Williamsburg the 19th of April last, Thomas SANDEFUR, a soldier in my company of state artillery, 40 years of age, 6 feet high, very slim, dark brown hair..and as he has relations living on New River, Onslow county, and fishing Creek, near Tarborough, have reason to believe he is lurking about either of those places. Fifty dollars..to have him delivered to the commanding officer in Williamsburg... Lawrence HOWSE, C. V. A.

(448) Stolen or strayed from Edenton about six weeks ago a fine black horse.. Also run away from said place about three months ago, a negro man named COLAS, born in the French West-Indies, and brought here some time in last war..40 years old, 5 feet 8 or 9 inches high.. was formerly the property of Mr. LASAILRE (?), a French gentleman, known in Newbern. Whoever delivers said negro and horse to Mess. LOWRY, in Newbern, Mon. LA PORTE, Edenton, Mr. John MEALS, Fredericsburg, Virg. or Galvan DE BERNOUGH, Fredericksburg, shall receive 60 dollars for the negro, and 40 dollars for the horse. Edenton July 28.

(449) Forty Dollars Reward. Run away from the subscriber the last of June, a negro girl named SUCK, of a low size..she lately belonged to Doctor LENOX, has a husband over the creek at Mr. JOHNSTON's, named BORTON... Bajieu LAPORTE.

(450) The subscriber, Doctor in Physick, and one of the first surgeons in the King of France's armies, gives the public notice of setting up in this town, to exercise the art of my profession..I possess the art of man midwife, I also undertake to cure all sorts of venereal distempers, ulcers, and ring worms. The poor people who may want assistance, I will attend gratis... PAMBRUSE. Edenton, July 28.

August 7, 1778. Number 440.

(451) Trenton, June 3. Extracts from his Excellency Governor LIVINGSTON's Message to the General Assembly of the State of New-Jersey... Wil. LIVINGSTON. Princeton, May 29.

(452) Newbern, August 7, 1778. Since our last, died here, after a very short illness, Mrs. Phebe OGDEN, wife of Mr. Thomas OGDEN, of this town; a lady in the bloom of youth and beauty...

(453) Advertisements. Craven, July 29, 1778. Whereas some busy body ..has propagated a report that Mr. William BLOUNT did intend offering himself a candidate at the late election in Newbern, for being a member to represent this county in the House of Commons..it was confidently asserted, at the election, that I had propagated the report.. whoever says he heard me say..that I thought Mr. BLOUNT intended..is a lyar... William BRYAN.

(454) Imported..from France, and to be Sold at public vendue, on Tuesday the 2d of September next, by SAVAGE and WESTMORE, at Edenton.. the following large Assortment of Goods...

(455) Was found in my field, in Craven county,..a bay horse.. The owner may have him by proving his property and paying charges. John HACKBURN.

August 14, 1778. Number 441.

(456) Wilmington District, June 11, 1778. To the Honorable Samuel ASHE, Esq; one of the Judges of the Superior Court of Law, Sir,...

(457) Advertisements. Newbern, August 11, 1778. Whereas my wife Katy has eloped from me, I take this public method to inform all persons from trusting her on my account, as I will not be answerable for any debts she may contract from the date hereof. James FLETT.

August 21, 1778. Number 442.

(458) Advertisements. Newbern, August 21, 1778. The subscriber takes this method of acquainting the public that James FLETT, (taylor of this town) hath unjustly traduced the character of his lawful, prudent, and virtuous wife-And he further adds, that he will be accountable for any transgression said FLETT can make evident against his wife.-Therefore he expects the public will consider said FLETT an unjust and cruel man, if he cannot prove any reason for acting in so vile a manner... John Horner HILL.

(459) Letters remaining in the Post-Office at Newbern, viz. One for Mrs. Fransina HARVEY, near Cox's Ferry. Mr. Francis HODGSON, sloop Sea Flour, 1 do., Mr. Dugald CAMBELL, Newbern, 1 do., Mr. William MECOY, Craven county,1 do., 5th July. Mrs. Judath DYER, Newbern, 1 do., 18th do., Mr. Archibald GILLESPIE, Bogue Inlet, 1 do., 25th do. Mr. Waightstill AVERY, Attorney General. Mrs. Judath DYER, Newbern, 1 do. 1st Aug. Mr. John STEEL, New River, 1 do. Major William FENNER, Newbern, 1 do., Capt. Jehiel TINKER, Newbern, 1 do., 7th do. Monsieur LISTRE, Newbern, 1 do., 8th do. Mr. John COWPER, Tar River, 1 do., 14th do. Mrs. Elizabeth WASHINGTON, Tar River, 1 do. Mr. William BLOUNT, 1 do. 19th do. Mr. Henry DIXON, Beaufort, 1 do. R. COGDELL, P. M.

August 28, 1778. Number 443.

(460) Williamsburg, August 14. The following is a true Copy of a Handbill written by Mr. MADUIT, under the direction of Lord HORTH, and circulated by order of Administration. Arthur LEE.

(461) Advertisements. Just Published, And to be sold at the Printing Office in Newbern, Price bound, Two Dollars: The Rudiments of the Latin Tongue.. By Tho. RUDDIMAN, M. A.

(462) Run away from the Subscriber in Onslow county, a negro man named PRIMUS, 5 feet 6 inches high, 27 years old.. Ten dollars reward... James FOY.

(463) State of North Carolina, Craven County, ss. By Richard ELLIS, and William TISDALE, Esquires, two of the Justices for the said County, Newbern, June 27, 1777. Whereas complaint hath been made to us, by James DAVIS, that a negro fellow named SMART, very black, about 5 feet 8 inches high, well made and very likely..is run away and is supposed to be lurking about, committing many acts of felony. These are therefore to command the said slave forthwith to surrender himself.. And we do..declare, if the said slave doth not surrender himself, and return home..that then any person may kill or destroy the said slave.. without accusation or impeachment of any crime... Richard ELLIS. William TISDALE. N. B. 'Tis supposed he is harboured about Core Sound.. I will give 50 dollars if delivered to me at Green Spring, or 20 dollars for his head. James DAVIS.

September 4, 1778. Number 444.

(464) Poughkeepsie, July 20. Since our last, many of the distressed refugees from the Wyoming settlement, on the Susquehannah, who escaped the general massacre of the inhabitants, have passed this way, from whom we have collected the following account, viz...this settlement was made by the people of Connecticut on a grant of Lands purchased by the inhabitants of that colony, under sanction of government, of the Indian proprietors, and that these lands falling within the limits of the Pennsylvania claim, a dispute concerning the right has arisen between the two governments, and proceeded to frequent acts of hostility:.the dispute has lain dormant for two or three years; the inhabitants lived happily, and the settlement encreased, consisting of eight townships, viz. Lackewana, Exeter, Kingston, Wilkesborough, Plymouth, Nanticoak, Huntington, and Salem, each containing five miles square. The settlement included upwards of a thousand families..besides the garrisons of four forts, in the townships of Lackewana, Exeter, Kingston, and Wilkesborough. - One of these forts was garrisoned by upwards of 400 soldiers, chiefly of the militia; the principal officers in which were colonels DENISON and Zebulon BUTLER. The Tories and indians had given some disturbance to those settlements last year, before general HARKENER's battle at Oneida creek, near fort Stanwix..the tories concealed themselves among our different settlements. About this time, the inhabitants having discovered that many of these villainous tories who had stirred up the Indians, and been with them in fighting against us, were within the settlements, 27 of them were..taken up and secured. Of these, 18 were sent to Connecticut; the rest..for want of sufficient evidence set at liberty.. On the 1st instant (July) the whole body of the enemy..of near 1600 (about 300 of them..indians..the rest tories painted like them, except their officers..) the whole under the command of colonel John BUTLER (a Connecticut tory, and cousin to colonel Zebulon BUTLER, the second in command in the settlement).. July 2. The enemy appeared on the mountains back of Kingston.. The same night..

76

(464) (Cont.) ..they took Lackewana fort, killed squire JENKINS and
his family.. July 4... Col. Nathan DENNISON went with a flag to Exeter fort, to know of Col. John BUTLER what terms he would grant on a
surrender.. Captains James BEDLOCK, Robert DURGEE, and Samuel RAN__,
(killed by fire). Thomas HILL (whose father was killed by the indian
last indi__ war) with his own hands killed his own mother, his father
in __w, his sisters, and their families. Partial TERRY..murdered his
fa__r, mother, brothers, and sisters, stripped off their scalps, and
___ off his father's head.

(465) New-York, August 5. On Monday morning about one o'clock, the
city was alarmed by a tremendous fire, which broke out at the house
of Mr. STEWART, at CROGER's dock..soon consumed all the buildings on
the east, south and west end of the said wharf.. The fire..soon
caught the back buildings in dock street, and burnt every house to
the east of Mr. Isaac LOW's as far as the old slip...

(466) Newbern, Sept. 4, 1778. Last week, Mr. Thomas BARKER arrived
at his house in Edenton, from France, and the next day waited on a
justice of the peace and took the oath of allegiance to this state.
Mr. BARKER has been absent about 17 years, during which time he has
resided in England...

(467) Advertisements. Newbern, Sept. 4. The subscriber informs the
public that he has lately arrived in town, where he intends to remain
until the 1st of November next, in order to settle all the affairs of
his late father John CLITHERALL, Esq;.. Doctor CLITHERALL intends to
dispose of all his landed property both in town and country in the
different parts of this state before his return to South Carolina...
James CLITHERALL.

(468) On Monday the 7th of September, will be hired out to the highest bidder, for one year, (at the late dwelling house of George Phiny
LOVICK deceased) a parcel of very likely negroes, belonging to the or
phans of the deceased...

(469) Whereas my wife Betty has eloped from me. I hereby forewarn
any person or persons trusting her on my account, as I shall not pay
any debts she may, after this date, contract. William HALES. Sept. 4

(470) To be sold at public Vendue at Beaufort.. The cargo of the
Mare de Famille, from Cadiz..salt, wines, raisons, and cloths...
Lory BROTHERS.

(471) Letters remaining in the Post-Office at Newbern. September
1st, 1778. Mr. Francis HODGSON, sloop Sea Flour. Mr. William MC COY
Craven county. Major William FENNER, Newbern, 2 letters. Capt. Jehiel TINKER, Newbern. Monsieur LISTRE, Newbern. Mr. Peter PAULET, t
the care of Mess. ASTON & BATCHELOR. M. Laurence JOYNER, Newbern.
Mr. James GATLIN, Neuse River. R. COGDELL, P. M.

September 11, 1778. Number 445.

(472) Philadelphia, August 11. Last Thursday being the day appointe
by Congress the sieur GERARD, minister plenipotentiary from his most
christian majesty...received audience accordingly, In pursuance of
the ceremonial established by Congress, the honourable Richard Henry
LEE, Esq; one of the delegates from Virginia, and the honourable Sam-

77

(472) (Cont.) uel ADAMS, Esq; one of the delegates from Massachusetts Bay; in a coach and six provided by Congress, waited upon the minister at his house.

(473) Baltimore, Aug. 18. The private letters of George JOHNSTONE, Esq; one of the British commissioners, to the honourable Joseph REED, and ___bert MORRIS, Esqrs. members of Congress, with Mr. REED's ___-laration, in his place, of the conversation and.offers of a lady ___ Philadelphia, in behalf of Mr. JOHNSTONE having..been taken into consideration by Congress.. Resolved, that the..said paragraphs..be considered as direct.attempts to corrupt and bribe ___ Congress of the united states of.America.

(474) To be sold at John Horner HILL's store opposite Richard ELLIS's Esq; Rum, molasses, sugar, coffee,...

(475) State of North Carolina. By his Excellency.Richard CASWELL,. Esquire, Governor... A Proclamation. Whereas the scarcity of provisions in this state renders it necessary to prevent the exportation thereof: I..issue this proclamation, hereby prohibiting the export-ation of beef, pork, bacon, flour, wheat, Indian corn, rice, peas, and every other kind of provision..within 30 days from the date here-of... Given at Newbern..the 9th day of September, Anno: Domini 1778.. Richard CASWELL. By his Excellency's Command, J. GLASGOW, Sec.

(476) To be sold at Beaufort, on Monday the 2d of November next..a large, valuable..assortment of goods, lately arrived in the ship Deane Capt. Bernard MARGOLLI, from France...

September 18, 1778. Number 446.

(477) New-York, August 5. "In the packet arrived..ensign William KENT, of the Devonshire militia volunteers: Dr. BECKENHOUT; Mr. John TEMPLE, of Boston, with his lady and family; Mr. John LEVI, partner. with Mr. SAMUEL, merchant of this city; Mr. HOGG and Mr. MARSHALL, of North Carolina; Mr. James GRAHAM, and Mr. William TELLFAIR, of London, merchants; Mr. TUNNO, late of South Carolina, merchant."

(478) Baltimore, August 25. The following is a copy of a letter from Mr. Henry FISHER to the honourable Navy Board, at Philadelphia, dated Lewis-Town, August 17, 1778...

(479) Advertisements. Newbern Sept. 18. The subscriber informs the public he disposes of all his lands..at private sale until Tuesday the 13th of October next.. One tract of 215 acres a little way out of town, one plantation upon Neuse river, about 1400 acres, four miles from Newbern..one tract about 1185 acres..on Trent; 28 miles from town one tract on the streights, Core Sound; Several tracts at Cross Creek; several tracts on Hammond Creek, and some other tracts in different parts of the country..lotts in Beaufort and Brunswick.. All those who have any demands against the estate of the late John CLITHERALL, Esq; deceased... James CLITHERALL.

(480) Whereas I gave a note to Mr. William LOW some time ago, which I have been ready to pay long since, but do not know who has the said

78

(480) (Cont.) note, as Mr. LOW has left this state; I therefore give this notice that I will not pay any interest for the same after this date. Sept. 18. William SPIGHT.

(481) Chowan County, Sept. 5. Run away from the subscriber the 31st of August last, a mulatto fellow named JACK, 25 years old, about 5 feet 7 inches high, well set, a blacksmith by trade.. Whoever delivers the said slave to me, near Edenton..or, if taken in this county, 30 dollars reward, if out of the county, 50 dollars and be entitled to what money he has with him when taken... John Bap. BEASLEY.

September 25, 1778. Number 447.

(482) Boston, August 13. The following is a copy of a letter from the honourable major general John HANCOCK, dated Rhode Island, August 11, 1778, to the honourable Jeremiah POWELL, Esq; president of the hon. council of this state...

(483) Philadelphia, August 29. Yesterday morning the noted highwayman James FITZPATRICK, blacksmith, sent up from Chester, on a warrant from the Chief _ustice, for the more secure confinement, was lodged in the public jail of this city. He is to be sent back for trial in due time.

(484) Extract of a letter dated camp at White Plains, August 24. "A few days ago GALLOWAY asked lieut. col. B___r (blank), who went in with a flag, if he thought there was a possibility of his getting to Philadelphia without losing his life... The enemy would not permit GALLOWAY or Dan. COX to speak to either of them without an officer being present."

(485) New-York, August 18. Extract from the journal of Mr. Alexander M_PHERSON, commander of the ship Elderslie of Glasgow...

October 2, 1778. Number 448.

(486) Newbern, October 2, 1778. Extract of a letter from General WASHINGTON to Congress, dated head quarters White Plains, Sept. 1. Sir, "I do myself the honour of transmitting you a copy of a letter I this moment received from general SULLIVAN.." Head Quarters, on the North end of Rhode Island, Aug. 29. Dear General,... John SULLIVAN.

(487) We are advised from Pitt County of the untimely death of Mr. Joseph WORSLEY, of that county, who on the 12th of Sept. received a kick from his horse, of which blow he expired in about three hours. Mr. WORSLEY was ever esteemed an honest, industrious, and respectable planter, a kind and beneficent neighbour, and a warm friend to his country. He has left a widow and many children, who severely bemoan his loss.

(488) Advertisements. Boyle ALDWORTH, Limbner. Just arrived in this town, paints likenesses on the following Conditions, viz. Portraits for rings, 130 Dollars, Do. for braceletts, 100 Dollars, Do. in crayons, as house ornaments from 1 to 2 feet, 75 Dollars.. N. B. Enquire

(488) (Cont.) for Mr. ALDWORTH at OLIVER's tavern. Newbern, Sept.29.

(489) Craven County, Oct. 1. To be sold at public sale on Thursday the 22d of October, at the late dwelling house of Moses ALMAND, deceased, on Brice's creek, all the stock..corn, wheat, and tobacco, and the house and kitchen furniture &c... Perrin ALMAND, Administrator.

(490) Letters remaining in the Post-Office at Newbern, September 15, 1778. Francis HODGSON, of the sloop Sea Flower; William MC COY, Craven county. Capt. Isaac BARTHOLOMEW, Beaufort. Mr. Daniel YEATS, on Trent River. Col. Jacob BLOUNT, near Newbern. William BLOUNT, Esq; 2 letters. Capt. Thomas BLOUNT, of the 5th N. C. regiment, 3 letters. Brig. Gen. Allen JONES, Halifax. Messieur J. D. KERN, merchant. Richard COGDELL, P. M.

October 9, 1778. Number 449

(491) Philadelphia, September 3, 1778. Letter from the Honourable Major General SULLIVAN to the President of Congress, dated Head-Quarters, Tiverton, August 31, 1778. Esteemed Sir, ... One regiment was posted in a redoubt advanced on the right of the first line; Colonel Henry B. LIVINGSTON with a light corps, consisting of Colonel JACKSON's detachment and a detachment from the army, was stationed in the east road; another light corps under the command of Colonel LAURENS, Colonel FLEURY, and Major TALBOT, was posted on the west road,.in the rear of those was the picket of the army, commanded by Colonel WADE,. The enemy advanced on our left very near, but were repulsed by General GLOVER..Colonel CAMPBELL came out the next day to gain permission to view the field of action, to search for his nephew, who was killed by his side, whose body he could not get off, as they were closely pursued.. Colonel LIVINGSTON, and all the officers of the light corps behaved with great gallantry. The brigades of the first line, VARNUM's, GLOVER's, CORNELL's, and GREEN's, behaved with great firmness.. Brig. Gen. LOVEL; he, and his brigade of militia, behaved with great resolution. Colonel CRANE, and the officers of artillery, deserve the highest praise.. The Marquis de la FAYETTE arrived about eleven in the evening from Boston.. Major MORRIS, one of my aids, will have the honour of delivering this to your Excellency,.. John SULLIVAN. P. S. .. Maj. TALBOT, who assisted in preparing the boats, afterwards served in Col. LAURENS's corps, deserves great praise.

(492) Advertisements. Twenty Dollars Reward. Ran away from me in Newbern, a negro woman named SALL, a short, thick, yellowish wench.. She has been seen in company with BILLICO, a fellow of Mr. SANDERS's, and is supposed harboured by him... Mary GORDON.

(493) For Sale, Two new cables 120 fathom each, one 9 inches, the other 11 inches French measure, equal to a 10 and 12 inch English cable, and suitable for a vessel of 200 tons burthen. .. apply to Mr. John W. STANLEY, or Messrs. Thomas and Titus OGDEN in Newbern.

(494) State of North Carolina, Beaufort County, ss. To the sheriff, constables, and all other officers of the said county. Whereas Sarah Blango MOORE (free negro) has this day made complaint to me, one of

(494) (Cont.) the justices for the county aforesaid, that she was
last night robbed of two of her own children, by three men in disguise
one a boy about six years old named AMBROSE, the other a girl named
ROSE, of the same age, they being twins; and that she hath just reason to suspect several ide and disorderly persons within your pre-
cincts to have taken the same. These are therefore in the name of
the State to command you..to search diligently within your respective
Bailiwicks for the said robbers, and to make hue and cry after them..
Given under my hand and seal this 11th September, 1778. Thomas BON-
NER.

October 16, 1778. Number 450.

(495) Williamsburg, October 2, 1778. To Mr. Alexander PURDIE.
(Letter-ending missing.)

(496) (Large portions of this item are missing.) Newbern, Octobe
To the Public. It gives me much pain to offer any thing ___ ___, but
when I find my character; ___ attacked, hope they will indulge me with
a vindicat___ On or about the 18th of August last, a certain ____
JAMES, of this county, received a violent stab in his bo__ __ __
cutlas from a Frenchman. Two or three days after, ___ that the
man was dead, search was made for the French___ ... On their not find·
ing him, Col. John ____ sheriff of this county, was told by several
gentlemen he had __ter advertise..as the likeliest way to apprehend
him, and offered among them to make up a reward of 20 pounds, of
which sum William TISDALE, Esq; offered to pay 10 pounds. Col. BRYAN
left them and said he would go to Mr. DAVIS and have it done immediately. In less than an hour Mr. John KENNEDY, gaoler and deputy sher·
iff came to the printing office, told me he was sent by Col. BRYAN to
order me to advertise the murderer, as JAMES was dead.. ..the orders
were obeyed, and an advertisement published.

At the last county court here, notwithstanding the above proceed·
ings, a prosecution against me was most violently urged, the printed
advertisement was found on the table of the foreman of the grand jury
and its supporters were soon discovered to be Col. Joseph LEECH, Dr.
GASTON, and Col. BRYAN himself, who had ordered the publication, as
his deputy told me. It was urged by them gentlemen that no such murder had been committed, ___ ___ Jeremiah JAMES died of ____ Mr.
TISDALE and some other persons proposed to have him advertised, and
promised to give any person 20 pounds reward, who would apprehend the
aforesaid Frenchman. This deponent further saith, that he desired
Colonel John BRYAN, sheriff of Craven county, to go home with him and
he would ___(Remainder missing)

November 7, 1778. Number 453.

(497) Baltimore, October 6. Extract of a letter from Capt. John BAR-
ROWS to his friend in this town, dated at Cape Francois, Sept. 12,
1778...

(498) Williamsburg, October 16. Intelligence from the south western
frontiers of this state. Col. CLARK, with a body of militia, has tak-
en possession of fort Chartres, and the other western posts between

(498) (Cont.) the rivers Ohio and Missisippi.. Capt. BOONE, the famous partisan, has lately crossed the Ohio with a small detachment of men, and near the Shawanese towns repulsed a party of the enemy.. Major SMITH has marched with three companies of the militia of Washington county to support the garrisons in Kentucky, The noted Cherokee Chief CHEU-CONNASCON, or DRAGGING CANOE, is lately dead...

(499) Advertisements. Wanted, To be delivered in Newbern, in Four Weeks, 800 barrels of tar, for which a generous price will be given by Lory BROTHERS. October 28, 1778.

(500) North-Carolina, Craven County, ss. Whereas I the subscriber James HOBBS, at a g neral muster in May last, did falsely accuse Capt. William RANDEL of getting his living by stealing hogs and cattle I do now declare and confess that the said accusation is false and groundless, and that I am now heartily sorry for having unjustly aspersed his character.. William RA DEL is a very honest, good man, and a good neighbour... Witnes my hand this 27th day of October, 1778. James HOBB . W. AVERY. Robert P. DALY.

(501) For Cadiz. The Ship la Mere de Famille, Pierre BEUTZ Master, now lying at Beaufort..for freight apply to said master at Beaufort (or) in Newbern to Lory BROTHERS.

(502) To Be Sold, To the highest bidder at Woodstock, the 10th day of Novemb next, for Ready Money, the sloop Adventure. Burthen about 40 tons... Capt. George DAMES.

(503) Whereas my wife Margaret has eloped from me, I hereby forewarn all persons trusting her __ my account, as I will not pay any debts she may hereafter contract. October 15. William WOOD.

November 14, 1778. Number 454.

(504) Boston, September 24. Last Monday returned into port, from a cruise, the private armed ship, General Hancock, lately commanded by Captain Ishmael HARDY. On the 9th instant, she fell in with the Levant English frigate, of 32 guns... At half past 2, Capt. HARDY received a wound in his right shoulder, by a musket ball, which lodged in the vertebrae of his neck; he fell, and was carried below. The first Lieutenant then took the command, and engaged broadside for broadside till 4 o'clock, when the Levant blew up...

(505) Fish-Kill, October 1. By a Gentleman from New Jersey we are informed that last Tuesday week between 5 and 8000 troops..under the command of General CORNWALLIS, arrived at the English neighbourhood from New York. On Wednesday morning they surprised a picket of militia stationed near that place, about 300 militia, under the command of Col. Gilbert COOPER, immediately collected, who drove off the cattle, and kept the ground within four miles of the enemy. On Sunday Col. BAYLOR's regiment of light horse arrived at Old Tappa,.. We hear young Mr. BOGART, son of Mr. Nicholas BOGART, of New York, was a few days ago inhumanly killed by the enemy in New Jersey.

(506) Baltimore, October 13. We hear from Philadelphia that a few

(506) (Cont.) days ago Abraham CARLYLE, once a reputable citizen, was found guilty of high treason at the court of Oyer and Terminer now sitting there.

(507) Advertisements. To be Sold at public auction, on Tuesday the 24th instant, for ready money, The Sloop Three Friends..now lying at Mr. John W. STANLY's wharf. An inventory may be seen by applying to the subscriber at Mr. WRENFORD's. Cornelius DIERANT, Jun. Nov. 12, 1778. (Note: 20 Nov. 1778 issue-name appears as Cornelius DURANT, Jun.)

(508) Fulling Mill. The subscriber acquaints the public that he has erected a Fulling Mill in Pitt county, about 10 miles above the Red Banks, where all..may be assured of having their cloths done in the best manner.. If materials can be procured, he can dye from a scarlet to a common drab. George WOLFENDEN. Pitt, Nov. 7, 1778.

(509) State of North Carolina, Craven County, ss. By Richard ELLIS and William TISDALE, Esquires, two of the Justices for the said County Newbern, June 27, 1777. Whereas complaint hath been made to us, by James DAVIS, that a negro fellow named SMART, very black, about 5 feet 8 inches high, well made, and very likely, speaks broken English, but very artful and insinuateing, is run away, and is supposed to be lurking about committing many acts of felony. These are therefore to command the said slave forthwith to surrender himself, and return home to his Master.. And we do hereby..declare, if the said slave doth not surrender himself, and return home..that then any person may kill or destroy the said slave..without accusation..of any crime... Richard ELLIS. William TISDALE. N. B. 'Tis supposed he is harboured about South River, by one Abel CARTER, a free negro, as he has been seen there several times. I will give 50 dollars if delivered to me at Green Spring or 20 dollars for his head. James DAVIS.

November 20, 1778. Number 455.

(510) Philadelphia, October 17. Extract of a letter from the Commissioners of the Navy Board at Boston, to the Marine Committee of Congress, dated the 7th of October. "This will inform you of the loss of the Raleigh frigate, commanded by John BARRY, Esquire... Capt. BARRY's conduct is highly approved here.." Published by order of the Marine Committee, John BROWN, Secretary.

(511) Williamsburg, November 6. The Information of Abraham WHILTBANK of Lewis-Town, Pilot, delivered to the President of Congress...

(512) A few days ago a flag of truce arrived in Hampton road with 14 passengers from New York, most of them late residents of this state, when only four of that number were permitted to return, viz. Dr. Charles MORTIMER, of Fredericksburg, Mr. Alexander TRENT, son of Col. Alexander TRENT of Cumberland county, Miss Elizabeth MUIR, who lately came from Great Britain to reside with her brothers in Alexandria, and Mr. DE BUTTS of Maryland.

(513) In the House of Delegates, Tuesday, November 3. Resolved, That Charles MORTIMER and Alexander TRENT be received into this commonwealt

(513) (Cont.) and that they take the oath of fidelity within 12 hours after their landing at Hampton. Resolved, That Elizabeth MUIR ought to be permitted to reside in this state. Resolved, That John DEBUTTS be permitted to pass through this state to Maryland, he having first taken the oath of fidelity... Resolved, That James GILCHRIST, Isaac HESLOP, Hardin BURNLY, Robert COWAN, William M'WHAN, Alexander BU H- ANAN, James M'DOWAL, Thomas MITCHEL, John PATTERSON, and Alexander CAMPBELL, be not admitted into this state, and that..the Governor be requested to give orders that the flag that brought them to Hampton road immediately depart this state with the said passengers.

(514) Last Monday morning the body of John SMITH, one of the orderly men at the state hospital, was found dead in the lower end of this city, supposed to have been murdered in the night.

(515) In the night of the 29th ult. Mr. Lockey COLLIER, of Elizabeth City county, was murdered in his bed by his own negroes, who strangled him...

(516) Advertisements. One Hundred Dollars Reward. Run away from the subscriber a Negro Fellow called ABRAHAM, a tall, slim, yellow fellow, lately the property of Mr. Peter STARKEY. Whoever will apprehend the said fellow, and have him secured in any gaol..shall receive 25 Pounds by applying either to me in South Carolina, or to General ASHE, at the North East; or the above reward to any person who will give informa- tion of his being harboured by a white man upon conviction... Wm. ALLSTON.

(517) Eighty Dollars Reward. Run away from the subscriber in Beau- fort, Carteret County, a negro wench named NAN... William BOURDEN.

(518) Newbern, November 19, 1778. To be Hired, on Saturday the 12th (?) December, for One Year..at the house of Mr. EMERY, Several very likely Negro fellows and wenches..by the administratrix of the estate of the Reverend Mr. James REED, deceased.

November 30, 1778. Number 456.

(519) Advertisements. 20 Dollars Reward. Strayed or stolen from the Subscriber in Newbern, last Monday, Two Horses... Richard COG- DELL. November 25, 1778.

(520) For Sale, The subscriber's valuable Plantation & Seat of Land in the county of Anson, North Carolina, about 25 miles from Cheraw Hill, in South Carolina, and extending within half a mile of Anson court-house, containing about 2000 acres, lying on Great Peedee river, ..a tolerable good dwelling house and kitchen with a brick chimney... Sam. SPENCER. November 24.

END OF REEL

The North Carolina Gazette 1783 - No issues Located.

1784 - All issues missing except for the following from Department of Archives and History-July 29. From American Antiquarian Society-September 2. From Historical Society of Pennsylvania-December 9.

The North Carolina Gazette or Impartial Intelligencer, and Weekly
General Advertiser. No.___
Among the useful Inventions of Man, there is none more to be admired
than the Art of Printing; by Means of which, useful Knowledge is communicated more easily, ___ expeditiously, than in any other Way;
therefore the Press ought ever to be encouraged and supported, particularly by Free Citizens, and Professing Christia__.

1784. Thursday, July 29.   Price Eight-pence.

(521) On the Reading Proper, for the Fair Sex. (Addressed to a
Young Lady, by the late Dr. SCHOMBERG.) ... J. SCHOMBERG.

(522) Newbern. Notice. For the better accomodation of the Gentlemen
of the approaching Assembly to be held at New-Bern, the subscribers
will have..at their plantation on Bachelor's Creek, seven miles from
Town, corn and other provender..to feed 100 Horses. No place can
have greater advantages of pasturage, being almost surrounded with
the Creek and River... Thos. and Titus OGDEN, Newbern, July 25th,
1784.

(523) The Executors of Robert HOGG, will be..obliged to the persons
indebted to that Estate for payment.. A Lot in Swansborough, with a
convenient House thereon,..to be sold. John HUSKE, Attorney. Wilmington, July 19th, 1784.

(524) State of North Carolina, Craven County. Whereas, complaint
hath been made to us, two of the Justices of the Peace for the County
aforesaid, by John ALLEN, Esq. that two Negro Slaves, one a man about
27 years of age named PRIMUS, about 5 feet 9 inches high, Country
born..the other a Boy, about 16 years of age, tall, and of a yellow
complexion, Country born, named TONEY, have absented themselves from
their said Master's service, and continue lurking about, committing
acts of felony.. And we do further notify that unless the said out-
lying Slaves,..do immediately..surrender themselves, that it shall be
lawful for any person..to kill and destroy the said..Slaves without
any impeachment of crime for so doing. Given under our hands, and
Seals, at New-Bern, this 23d day of July, Anno Dom. 1784. Richard
ELLIS, J. P., Joseph LEECH, J. P. A Reward of 10 pounds, will be
paid for each of the said Slaves if taken alive, or the same if they
be killed. John ALLEN.

(525) All persons indebted to the estate ___ ___ ___ John OWENS, deceased, are hereby requested to pay their respective ballances to the
subscribers, who are provided with the books and bonds, and properly
authorized to give discharges. Thos. and Titus OGDEN, Executors.
New-Bern, July 24th, 1784.

(526) Newbern, Post-Office, 15th July, 1784. Letters remaning in
this Office. 1 Caleb C. GOAH, 1 Doct. MC CLURE, 1 William TEMPLE,
Beaufort, 1 John SMITH, Beaufort, 1 Samuel COOPER Beaufort, 1 John
LAMBERT, 1 John NARLCUT, 1 Capt. WHITNEY, 1 Capt. VANCISE, 1 Joseph
EVERITT, up. Nuse, 1 Thomas COB, at Kingston, 1 Capt. A. ARMSTRONG,

(526) (Cont.) 1 Mr. SHAWICK, 1 Major John MC CLURE, 2 Saluthiel HEN-
DRICKSON, 1 John Council BRYAN. 1 John EASTON, 1 Dederick GIBBLE, 1
Mrs. Alevy SINGLETARY, 1 Capt. COTTER, at present in New-Bern, 1 Wil-
liam JOHNSTON Esq; Merchant at Hillsborough, 1 Reuben BUNKER, at New
Garden, Gilford County, 1 Benjamin RIDING, Nues River, near Smiths
Creek, 1 Capt. Benj. WILLIAMS, Johnston County, Nues River. R. COG-
DELL, P. M.

(527) Reward. Ran-Away, from the subscriber in Newbern..a Negro Fellow by the name of JOE, about 4 feet 10 inches high.. He is supposed
to be gone to South Carolina, in company with a Negro fellow, of Mr.
Silas STEVENSON... Abner NEALE, Newbern, July 15th, 1784.

(528) The Public Is solicited to a subscription for a French Gazette,
under the title of the Courier de l'Amerique... Said Paper printed
by Charles GIST, in Philadelphia, for the Proprietors, BOINOD and
GAILLARD. N. B. Subscriptions taken, in Newbern, by the Printer
hereof, Robert KEITH.

(529) To Be Sold, by Solomon HALLING, opposite to Mr. John GREEN's,
in Front-Street;.. A General assortment of Drugs, Medicines, &c im-
ported in the last Vessels which have arrived at Philadelphia from
Europe. Antimony, Allum, AEther, Brimstone, Copperas, Calomel Ppt.,
Corrosive Sublimate, Cantharides, Chamomile Flowers, Dragon's Blood,
Essence of Lemon's, Bergamot, Flowers of Sulphur, Glauber's Salts,
Gum: Aloes Socotorine, Barbadens, Camphor, Arabic, Assafoetida, Guai-
acurn, Ammoniac; Juniper Berries, Lapis Calaminaris, Laudanum Liquidum
Manna, Magnesia Alba, Mercurial Ointment, Nitre, Oatmeal, Oil of Anise,
Carraway, Lavender, Mint, Vitriol, Pearl Barley, Powder of Jalap, Rhu-
barb, Peruvian Bark, best, Ditto, in Powder, Roman or Blue Vitriol,
Red Praecipitate, Root of Gentian, Jalap, Liquorice, Rhubarb, Sarsa-
parilla, Sal. Volat. Ammon, Salt of Tartar, Wormwood, Spirits of Nitre,
Hartshorn, Lavender Compound, Volat. Aromatic, Senna Leaves, Spanish
Liquorice, Sugar of Lead, Sweet Oil, best, Traumatic Balsam, Turner's
Cerate, Tartar Emetic, White Vitriol, Spices... Patent Medicines-An-
derson's Pills, Daffy's Elixir, Essence of Peppermint, Stoughton's
Bitters, Turlington's Balsam... Newbern, July 22d, 1784.

(530) For the term ___ ___ public auction, on the third day of next
September, Craven Court, two unimproved Lots, in the Town of New-Bern,
on Broad Street, numbered 249, and 250; each..will be divided into
two equal parts, and leased in separate Tenements; at the same time,
and for the same term of years..four other unimproved Lots..numbered
313 on New Street, and Lots..327,328, and 329, on Handcock and Johnston Streets. By order of the Incorporated Society, for promoting and
establishing the New-Bern Academy. John SITGREAVES, Secretary. Newbern, July 15th, 1784.

(531) All persons indebted to the late Trustees, for promoting and
establishing the public School in New-Bern, are hereby requested to
make immediate payments, to William MC CLURE Esq; treasurer of the
incorporated Society, for promoting and establishing the New-Bern
Academy.. By Order &c. John SITGREAVES, Secretary. Newbern, July
15th, 1784.

(532) _____ Mr. DRY, by deed from Michael CLARK. 640 Acres, on the head of New River, between lands formerly the property of Joseph WILLIAMS and William LAWS, pattented to William MILLS, or Joshua MILLS, heir at law to said William MILLS, and by the said Joshua MILLS conveyed to John THALLEY, and by him sold and conveyed to Mr. DRY.

In Duplin County, 640 Acres, on Maxwell's Swamp, originally pattented to Eleazer ALLEN Esq. by his Executors sold to John THALLEY, and by him to Mr. DRY. Which several Tracts of Land,..will be sold.. At the same time and place,..some L___ in New Bern, and the Lands adjoining ____ Town that belongs to Mr. DRY's Estate... Benjamin SMITH Executo_... Blue Banks, June 26, 1784.

(533) All persons indebted t_ ___ Estates of the honorable ____am DRY, and John ROWA_ deceased, are once more ___ to settle... Benjamin SMITH, Exe_____. Blue Banks, June 16th, 1784.

(534) To Be Leas__. For any term not exceeding three ye___. Lots of Land adjoining the Town o_ ____rough, belonging to the Estate of Archi____ _____PIE Esq; late of Onslow County, dece___. And as some of the __ encroachments have been lately made ___ ___perty of the Orphans of said GILLESPI · forbid any person from committing ___ abuse on the said Lots... James GILLESPIE. July 16, 1784.

(535) We the subscribers, being appointed by the last County Court, Inspec___ of Tobacco, for the Town of New-__n.. Thomas L. CHEEKE. Samuel CHAPMAN. New-Bern, July 13th, 1784.

(536) The Subscriber, Fencing and Dancing Master, from Paris, acquaints Gentlemen and Ladies of New-Bern..a suitable encouragement ma be _____ him, will open a school at the Palace... John MARTIN.

(537) To Be Sold. __ the subscriber, that..well known plantation of the Forks, ___ three miles below Wilmington on _ W. River, containing about six ___ acres of Tide Swamp,the great___ ___ of which is upon Eagle's Island... Joseph EAGLES. Brunswick County, June 25th, 1784.

(538) The subscriber has just opened, at his store on Swifts Creek, an assortment of Goods suitable for the present season... John BRYAN Swifts-Creek. July 19, 1784.

(539) ____ to me to make immediate payment, but finding little attention has been paid to that notice..think it necessary..to inform them again, that after the 10th day of August next, all who neglect to dis charge their respective ballances may depend upon suits..against them Wilson BLOUNT. Newbern, July 20th, 1784.

(540) Twelve Pounds Reward. Ran away from the subscriber, a Negro Wench, named FAN, about 20 years of age, she is black, tall and big with child, or has one since she went away. Six Pounds reward..for committing her to any goal.. The same reward..for securing a Negro Fellow, named WILL, about 40 years of age, who ran away with her, by Alderson ELLISON. Bath, June 28th, 1784.

(541) Malcolm GILLIES, Lately from Europe, has for sale, at the hous

(541) (Cont.) of Dr. MC CLURE, in Newbern, an assortment of Goods..
Hardware, Jewelry, Scotch Lawns... Newbern, July 7th, 1784.

(542) ___ Bern: Printed for R. KEITH and Company, near the Church,
where Subscriptions, at Three Dollars per ___ m (Half of said Sum in
Advance) Essays, Articles of Intelligence, &c. for this Gazette, are
gratefully received. - Ad___ sements, of no greater Length than
the Breadth of a Column, are inserted Three Weeks for one Dollar, and
for every ___ s Continuance after, one Fourth of a Dollar; those of a
larger Size are inserted in the same Proportion.

September   No. 50
1784. Thursday, September 2.

(543) To the Printer of the North-Carolina Gazette. Sir, Your pub-
lishing the following may be of service to some of your readers, and
fulfill my promise to the Captain of a Sloop of War. I am Sir, Your
most obedient, John ALDERSON. July 15th, 1784...

(544) Newbern, September 2. On the 20th and 21, ult. was held the
annual Election in this town, when James COOR, Esq. was elected senator; Spyers SINGLETON Esq. for the town, and William BRAYAN and William BLOUNT Esqrs: for the County, Commoners.

(545) Thirty Dollars Reward. Ran-away from the subscriber, the 15th
day of May last, a Likely Negro Fellow, named SCRUB, About 25 years
old..of a middle stature.. I have owned him for 13 years past.. I
expect he will attempt to get to Norfolk (where he was raised) and
pass as a free man by the name of Charles THOMPSON, or Charles FRY...
Richard BENNEHAM. Orange County, August, 1784.

(546) Strayed or Stolen, From Coll. PALMER's at Bath..two Bay Horses
.. A reward of 20 Dollars..on delivery of said Horses to Coll. PALM-
ER at Bath, to Captain MEDICE at Woodstock, or to me in Halifax.
Thomas GILCHRIST. July 20th 1784.

(547) Newbern District-Superior Court of Law and Equity. The Clerks
of the several County Courts of Carteret, Beaufort, Dobbs, Hyde, Johnston, Wayne and Jones, are notified to call and receive their copies
of the last acts of the general assembly of this state. Silas COOKE.
Clerk's-Office, August 20 1784.

(548) Notice. That the Gentlemen of the approaching Assembly, might
be well accomodated with provender for their Horses, the Subscribers
did advertise they would provide Corn and other provender sufficient
for 100 head... Thos. and Titus OGDEN. New Bern 19th August 1784.

(549) A Purse of 100 Golden Guineas, To be run for, at the Town of
Washington, State of North-Carolina, on the last Wednesday in November
.. All Horses &c. to be entered with Richard BLACKLEDGE Esq. of Wash-
ington.. Five Guineas entrance money... Washington, August 16th 1784.

(550) Cheap. The subscriber has just received from New-York, by the
Schooner Ferebe, the following goods..to sell, as he will leave this
Town in a few days, by said vessel.. Frederick GUION. New Bern, Sep-,
tember 1st 1784.

(551) Notice, Is hereby given to all persons with whom I have open accounts, to bring them in..that they may be adjusted and settled. As I intend to embark ___ Europe in a short time, and as my return will be very uncertain, I leave my brother Henry Batts COOPER, fully authorized to settle, and carry on my business, in my absence. John COOPER. Washington, August 24th 1784.

(552) Forty Pounds Reward, Ran-Away from the subscriber, last night, a Negro man named WILL QUACK, a native of this country, is about 30 years of age, well set, about 5 feet 9 inches high... Richard BLACK-LEDGE. Washington, August 29th 1784.

(553) For Sale, My Houses and Lotts in Halifax..the dwelling house.. is..on a rising ground in the main street, commanding a prospect of the whole Town. 400 Acres of Land, about one mile and a half from Hillsborough.. My House and Lot in Washington.. My Houses in Halifax may be purchased at private sale by applying to Col. Wm. R. DAVIE ..so may my house and Lot in Washington... Joseph KIDD. Washington, August 25th 1784.

(554) Notice, Is hereby given to the Public,..that the Ferry on Neuse-River which I have had attended for some time past, is rated so very low by the County Court, as to put it entirely out of my power to give any further attendance thereto. John SMITH. New-Bern, August 11th 1784.

(555) If any descendant of Miriam ROGERS, the wife of Joseph ROGERS, late of Chowan County, State of North Carolina, yeoman, is now alive, and will apply to the subscribers, he or she may hear of something very advantageous. The above named Mirriam was the daughter of Capt. Joseph TODD, of South Hapton parish in the Island of Bermuda, and having married the said Joseph ROGERS, they removed to the State of Virginia, and thence to Chowan County in the State of North Carolina. Any person who can point out the time when and place where the last descendant of the above family departed this life (in case they are all dead) will confer a considerable obligation on John MALLERY, and Mallery TODD. State of Virginia, Isle of Wight County, 18th July 1784

(556) Notice. The subscriber intending very shortly to leave this Town, wishes all those who are indebted to him, would make immediate payment... Frederick RAMCKE. New-Bern, August 4th, 1784.

(557) Notice. For the better accomodation of the Gentlemen of the approaching Assembly, to be held at Newbern,..the subscriber will have provided at his plantation, Sportsmans-Hall, on Trent, two miles from Town, Corn and other provender sufficient to feed any number of horses... Gentlemen arriving in Town, and sending their Horses to M. Joseph OLIVER's, will find an hostler appointed to receive them, by John MOOR. New-Bern, August 3d, 1784.

(558) My Wife Elizabeth having absconded from my bed and board, I hereby forewarn all persons from trusting her on my account, as I am determined not to pay any debts of her contracting after the 19th of August 1784. William LAWSON. New-Bern, August 17th 1784.

1784.   Numb. 685.
The N. Carolina Gazette.
With the latest advices foreign and domestic. Influenced by All
Parties, But Restrained By None.
Thursday, December 9.

(559) New-Port, October 9. Monday last arrived at Providence the
ship Gen. Washington, from London, Capt. SMITH has brought with him a
large Bell, weighing 2500 lb., and a Clock, for the Baptist Meeting
House in that town.

(560) New-York, October 15. The following is copied from a late
Baltimore Paper. ..Mr. James RUMSEY (late of this town) having..a
mechanic discovery,..hath at length obtained, not only the approbation
of General WASHINGTON, but of General WOOD, the Hon. Mr. RANDOLPH of
the Council, D. GRA ... Certificate. I Have seen the Model of Mr.
RUMSEY's boat, constructed to work against the stream, ..my own opinion that he has discovered the art of working boats by mechanism, and
small assistance, against rapid currents, that the discovery is of
vast importance.. Given under my hand at the room of Bat_ county
in the state of Virginia, the 17th of September, 1784. George WASH-
INGTON.

(561) All persons indebted to the estate of Mr. David BARRON, deceased..as the executors are called on for a settlement of their accounts this present month, at the next court for the county of Craven..
The Executors. Newbern, Dec. 3, 1784.

(562) (Item illegible) Michael FALVEY. Phillip REILLY. Washington,
_____ 1784.

(563) We ___ ___ both here and at Tarborough, will be transacted and
carried on under the firm of REILLY and TUTON. Phillp REILLY. Oliver
TUTON. Washington, Nov. ___, 1784.

(564) For Sale, 1,100 Acres of Land, on the Double Creeks of Hyco,
Whereon are a saw-mill and grist-mill..the terms by applying to Mr.
POLLIAM (?), Greensville county, Virginia, to Mr. Wm. WAITE, on the
premises, or to the subscriber... Robert DICKINS. Caswell County,
Nov. 24.

(565) New-Bern: Printed for Thomas DAVIS, Printer to the Honourab'e
the General Assembly of this State, at the Print__ Office near the
Church, where Articles of Intelligence and ___ will be gratefully
received. - Advertisements of a moderate Length inserted for Five
Shillings the first Week, and Two (?) for each Week after; but double
if sent without the Money.

1785 - All issues missing except for the following from Department of
Archives and History-November 3.

1785 The Noth. Carolina Gaze___ or New-Bern Adverti___.
Thursday, Nov. 3.

(566) Advertisement. North-Carolina, New-Bern District. To Be Sold

(566) (Cont.) At Public Vendue..at the Court House in the county of
Craven the 15th December next. One half part the front of lot No. 8
situated in the Town of New-Bern, in front street, extending in said
street 26 feet, and back from the said street to the river Neuse, im-
proved with a Still-House in which are two stills, late the property
of Samuel CORNELL Esq. Two tracts..of land, each..640 acres..in the
county of Craven on Brice's creek on the Miry Savannah, late the property of William BRIMAGE. One other tract..of..640 acres..on Ellis's
Lake, late the property of the said William BRI_AGE. A mortgage right
in and ___ lots situated in th ___ with interest from the said date
from John COOK Esq; to Martin HOWARD formerly chief justice of this
province now State of North Carolina.. One other tract..in the county
of Craven, on the west side of Mosley's creek, beginning at WEST's
line from thence with the creek to GRIFFEN's line..thence to WEST's
line..to the first station..100 acres, late the property of Richard
TIER. One other tract of..200 acres..in..Craven, on the north side
of Neuse river and on Popular branch, joining WINSON's land, it being
the property of Thomas BROWN. One other parcel..in..Craven..40 acres,
joining Richard BLACKLEDGE's land on Mosley's creek, the late property
of Richard TIER.

     Will be sold as above, on the 19th of December, at the Court
House in the county of Beaufort, viz. One tract..lying in the county
of Beaufort north side of Pamptico river and east side of Town creek,
..245 acres, the late property of Robert PALMER. One other tract..in
the county of Beaufort, north side of Pamptico river and east side of
Goose creek..128 acres the property of Robert PALMER. Three 1___ __
the town of Bath _____ (Remainder missing.)

(567) Just Imported by Fras. LOWTHORP, and now opening at his Store,
opposite the Church, in New-bern, A fresh and general Assortment o_
Merchandize.

(568) Whereas I am informed, that frauds are daily committed by persons selling with false weights and measures, I hereby give notice to
all..in the county of Craven, forthwith to produce their weights and
measures to the standard, under the penalty by law inflicted. Henry
PURSS. New-Bern; Nov. 2d 1785.

(569) New-York, Sept. 17. Last Wednesday arrived at Philadelphia in
the ship London packet, capt. TRUXTON his excellency doctor FRANKLIN,
late Minister Plenipotentiary from the united states of America to the
court of France, after an absence of near nine years.. With the doctor came his two grandsons, Mr. Temple FRANKLIN and Master Benjamin

---

(570) Twenty-Five Dollars Reward. Absconded from New-Bern about 12
months past, a mulatto man slave named JOHN, who passes for a free
man and calls himself John MC CLISH..he has been seen at the plantation of the late George LOVICK, nine miles below New-Bern, on Neuse
river... Tho. WILLIAMS. New-Bern, Nov. 2d 1785.

(571) Newbern Academy. The incorporated Society for promoting and
establishing the Newbern Academy,..have now provided the Academy with
a gentleman properly qualified to superintend the education of youth,

(571) (Cont.) Mr. Samuel CHANDLER of the University of Cambridge..
Those who wish to be admitted as scholars, are desired to apply to
Mr. Wm. M'CLURE, or to the subscriber... By Order of the Society.
John SITGREAVES, Sec'y. Newbern, Oct. 24th.

(572) James JUHAN Gives notice that He intends to carry on the Bak-
ing Business, at his house in Craven-street, opposite Mrs. MARSHALL's
... New-Bern, Nov. 2d.

(573) The Subscriber gives notice, that he will strictly prosecute
any person whatever, that shall be found hunting or gunning, on his
lands near New-Bern, without his special leave. John SMITH.

(574) To be Sold, By J. CHAPONEL at his store nearly opposite the
Palace: A quantity of Rum, Sugar, Coffee, Melasses, vin de Grave and
Castile soa_...

1786 - No issues located.

1787 - All issues missing except for the following from the University
of Chicago-August 1. From American Antiquarian Society-August 15.
From Louisiana State Museum-July 11, December 19.

MARTIN's North-Carolina Gazette.
(Vol. II.) Newbern, July 11, 1787. (No. 80.)

(575) New-York, June 15. A melancholy accident happened on the third
instant, at the house of Major William BALLARD, who lately removed
from Amesbury, in the state of Massachusetts Bay, to Warner, in the
state of New-Hampshire. - A little girl, daughter to Major BALLARD,
who with other children, was left at home, while the rest of the
family went to attend divine service, it is supposed, carried a coal
of fire into a chamber where there were some shavings, which, taking,
soon communicated the flames to the whole house, which..with the un-
happy girl, was soon consumed..the distressed parents had buried an
elder sister to the deceased but a few days before...

(576) Norfolk, July 4. On Monday afternoon..lightning..set fire to
a warehouse belonging to Mr. Cornelius CALVERT.

(577) Married at Warrenton on Wednesday the thirteenth ult. Dr. James
Gloster BREHON to the amiable Miss Mildred WILLIS.

(Vol. II.) Newbern, August 1, 1787. (No. 83.)

(578) A Blacksmith, Who is thoroughly acquainted with his business,
will meet with constant employment, on generous terms by applying to
John ALDERSON... Pengo, July 20 ____

(579) For Sale and now ready to be launched, at Bogue, A New Vessel..
Titus OGDEN, V. M. July 24.

(580) Mrs. BRUIN Has the honour to inform the public that..she has
taken the house lately occupied by Dr. SMALLWOOD, in Front street,
where she now keeps a French School. She also undertakes to instruct

(580) (.Cont.) a few young ladies in all kinds of Needle and Dresden work..Drawing &c. She cleans the teeth to perfection and places new ones so perfectly as to deceive the sharpest eye. She possesses a speedy and infallible remedy for the Fever and Ague. She cures all the diseases of the Eyes.. She flatters herself the discerning public will pay no kind of attention, to any malicious reports her enemies may circulate to her disadvantage. July 5.

(581) Lost. The Certificates hereafter mentioned for which a reward of 20 per cent..Number 220, H. E. G. CASWELL, late Comptroller Ŀ90 8, Hon. MARTIN & R. D. SPAIGHT. Speak, S. & C. in 1785, Ŀ32, Number 481 HAWKS & COOR, Audit. of Newbern District, Ŀ29 10...

(582) Twelve Shillings, Per Bushel for Flax Seed, and Three Sh. & Four Pence, Per lb. for Bees Wax, Will be given in cash, by COLE & STEVENSON, at their store, in Newbern...

(583) Proposals for printing by subscription A new Edition of The Office and Authority of a Justice of the Peace.. Subscriptions are taken in at my office and at Messieurs HODGE & BLANCHARD's in Newbern .. MARTIN. Newbern, July 11th.

(Vol. II.) Newbern, August 15, 1787. (No. 85.)

(584) Philadelphia, July 27. We learn..that attempts have been made in England, to counterfeit the paper emissions of the United States, particular those of North and South Carolina; and that a certain Robert MUIR, or MURE, a native of Scotland, has been apprehended and committed to jaol in Portsmouth.

(585) Newbern, August 15. Died) on the 4th Instant, at the seat of Edward STARKEY, Esq; in Onslow county, Mr. Thomas OGDEN of this town.

(586) Five Pounds Reward. Ran away from the subscriber, in Jones County near Trenton, on the 21st of July; A Negro Wench named CLOE; aged 23 years, 5 feet 7 or 8 inches high, very black... Joseph REA-SONOVER. August 10, 1787.

(587) To Be Rented, That commodious and pleasantly situated Dwelling House, the property of Mrs. Mary EDWARDS, on Water street, fronting the river Neuse..apply to the subscriber in Newbern. Nathan SMITH. July 7.

(588) Whereas several counterfeited certificates of the Auditors for the counties of Anson, Richmond and Montgomery have been taken in pay-ment for goods,..at ARMSTRONG & MOUNTFLORENCE's store, in Franklin county, from a certain Jesse BOWERS, now in Halifax jail..they re-quest all persons who have had such certificates from them..if counter feited, to return them as soon as possible, either to Andrew ARMSTRONC in Louisburg Franklin county, or to James Cole MOUNTFLORENCE, in War-renton, who will give good ones in lieu thereof... And. ARMSTRONG. J. C. MOUNTFLORENCE. August 8.

(589) Commission Store. A. H. ADAMS respectfully informs the Gent-lemen of Newbern..that he has opened a Commission store, in Pollock-street...

(590) For Sale. A very valuable tract of land containing about 720 acres, lying on both sides of Richland-Creek in the Counties of Wake and Franklin (the latter formerly Bute) within about 50 miles of Tarborough, and near about the same distance from Fayetteville... Jonathan DAVIS. N. B. The subscriber lives near Warrenton.

(Vol. II.) Newbern, December 19, 1787. (No. 103.)

(591) Boston, November 3. The following letter, on the subject of the American constitution from the hon. Eldridge GERRY, Esq; one of the delegates representing this commonwealth in the late federal convention... E. GERRY. (to) The Hon. Samuel ADAMS, Esq; President of the Senate, and The Hon. James WARREN, Esq; Speaker of the House of Representatives of Massachusetts.

(592) Philadelphia, Nov. 29. Last Wednesday 61 members of the convention met at the State House and chose for their President the honourable Frederick Augustus MUHLENBERG. A correspondent says, his Excellency John JAY, ..who was at first carried away with the new plan of government, is now decidedly against it...

(593) We are happy in informing the gentlemen of the ancient and honorable society of Free and accepted Masons that the convention for electing the Grand Masters and Grand Officers for this state, met at Tarborough on Saturday the 9th inst. and made choice of the following gentlemen, to form the Grand Lodge of the state of North Carolina, for the year 1788. Samuel JOHNSON, Esq; Grand Master. His Excellency Richard CASWELL, Esq; deputy Grand Master, Richard ELLIS, Esq; Grand Senior Warden. Michael PAYNE, Esq; Grand Junior Warden. Abner NEALE, Esq; Grand Treasurer. The Honourable James GLASGOW, Esq; Grand Secretary. On Wednesday in the afternoon, Samuel JOHNSON, Esq; ..was elected Governor of this state.

(594) Extract of a letter from Tarborough Wednesday Dec. 12, 1787. On Saturday the nomination for a governor took place, Alexander MARTIN, Samuel JOHNSTON, John WILLIAMS (the Judge), William Richardson DAVIE and William BLOUNT were named, The first upon inquiry was found ineligible..the name of Richard Dobbs SPAIGHT was then inserted ..Samuel JOHNSTON is chosen.

(595) Committed to the gaol of this district a Run-away negro man who calls himself JACK, and says he is the property of Thomas JERDEN of Pungo. He is 45 years of age and about 5 feet 6 inches high... William DUDLEY. Dec. 19.

(596) Newbern Post-Office To be let to the lowest bidder the conveyance of the mail from this office to Wilmington, on horse back, for one year... H. MACHEN, P. M. Dec. 1.

(597) The subscribers have lately removed from their store on the County-Wharf, to the corner store next door to Messrs. COLE & STEVENSON... TAGERT ROSS & TAGERT. Dec. 4.

(598) Whereas, a few y____ ago, I gave my note o_ __ligation to the executors of ____ LOVICK for thirty odd barri_ __ orn, for the pay-,

(598) (Cont.) ment of w____ Mr. William HERRITAGE was _ecurity;.. have faithfully discharged ___ whole amount of said note..the holder of it refuse___ ncel it..do hereby forwarn..from receiv___ or taking an assignment of..said note... Henry PURS_. Dec. 29.

(599) For sale at James CARNEY'_ best Bordeaux Claret in bottles, and by the hogsh___. Oct. 31.

(600) The Western Post will start o_ _____ay. Letters remaining in the Off__ Joseph GERMAN, head of ___, Phillip KOWLES, Beaufort c___ (Remainder missing.)

1788 - No issues located.

1789 - No issues located.

1790 - All issues missing except for the following from American Anti-quarian Society-April 1, 15.

The North-Carolina Gazette.
(Vol. 5.) Thursday, April 1, 1790. (No. 221.)

(601) Hyder Ali Is now in high order, and will stand, for the last time, at Milton, the plantation of the subscriber, at Batchelor's Creek, on the main road to Kemp's ferry, on Neuse river... Wilson BLOUNT. march 3.

(602) A Subscription for a medal of General WASHINGTON. .. Subscrip-tions for the town and District of Newbern, will be received at the Post-Office, by F. X. MARTIN, Post-Master. Or any gentleman may have any number of medals sent to any part of the continent, by sending his order..to J. MANLY, to the care of Robert PATTON, Esq; Post-Master Philadelphia. Copy - We, the undersigned, have seen the Medal of Gen-eral WASHINGTON, and think it a strong and expressive likeness...Thom-as MIFFLIN, Governor of the State of Pennsylvania, Richard PETERS, Speaker of the House of Assembly. Christian FEBIGER, Treasurer of the State. Francis JOHNSTON, Colonel of the late American army.

(603) Pilgrim Will stand the ensuing season one half the time at New-bern and the other half at Trent Bridge... Robert HUNT. February 20.

(604) James M'KINLAY, intending to go to Europe on or before the 20th of next month, desires all persons having any demands against him to send their accounts immediately for payment..bonds with approved secu-rity will be required, as all accounts..not settled..will be left in the hands of John SITGREAVES, Esq. to be sued for. April 1.

(605) Newbern, April 1. The Hon. John SEVIER, Esq; is elected one of the Representatives of this state in the Congress of the United States for the Western Division.

(606) Having room to believe that Mr. John SIMPSON, of the town of Newbern, merchant, will offer for sale the right which he pretends to have to a certain plantation, lying in Johnson county, of which he holds a mortgage from Richard BLACKLEDGE, and upon which he has lately

(606) (Cont.) caused several executions issued in his favor, from the office of the clerk of the county court of Pitt, against the property of said BLACKLEDGE, to be levied; I have been..and am still in possession of said plantation-..have an indisputable title thereto.. and will not relinquish it, untill compelled by law. Ben. WILLIAMS. March 4.

(607) John SIMPSON assures the public he is not conscious of ever having given Col. Ben WILLIAMS reason to entertain any illiberal suspicions-that he has the best room to believe Col. WILLIAMS once divested himself of the property alluded to, and that he thinks it was put out of the power of mr. R. BLACKLEDGE legally to divest himself or invest Col. WILLIAMS in the lands... March 18.

(608) Strayed or stolen from the subscriber a likely young roan horse... Thomas HILL. Wilmington, March 25.

(609) Stolen five large silver tea Spoons and a pair of silver shoe Buckles; the spoons marked NS and stampt WT. Twenty shillings reward ... Ann STEVENSON. March 26.

(610) Pursuant to an Act of Assembly, will be Sold to the highest bidder, on Monday the 26th of April next, on the premises, within the Borough of Norfolk, That valuable Square of Land whereon the late County Court-House is erected..on the main street, contiguous to the market-house, and county wharf... William NEUSUM, Robert BUTT, James WEBB, Edward ARCHER, John HODGES, jun. Com'rs. Norfolk, Feb. 4, 1790

(611) For Sale, The following property in the town of Newbern, to wit. The eastern half of the lot no. 13, lying on the north side of front street, between the old coffee-house and Richard ELLIS, Esq's. The lot no. 52..that part..at present occupied by Messrs. COLE and STEVENSON having 50 feet six inches front on Craven street and 107 feet three inches on Pollock street-that part occupied by Mr. William LAWRENCE,...also the premises occupied by Mr. A. WILLIS having 100 feet front on Craven street.. The lot no. 57, on the west side of Craven street between Capt. FORBES's and mrs. GASTON's... Richard Dobbs SPAIGHT. January 12.

(612) William BECKING & Co. At their stores in Pollock-street and on the County-wharf, have for sale, a large..assortment of European, East and West-India and American manufactured Goods, which they will sell on the most reasonable terms, as the above partnership will be dissolved on the 20th of next month.

(613) Notice is hereby given to all persons who have demands against the copartnership of William BECKING & co. or against the estate of William BECKING (late of Newbern, merchant dec.) to send in their accounts to the subscriber... Christopher Lewis LENTE. Only surviving Partner of W. BECKING & co. February 4.

(614) Pink Root For Sale by Solomon HALLING. April 1.

(615) Newbern: Printed by F. X. MARTIN.

(616) List of letters remaining in the Post-Office, Newbern, April 5, 1790. Thomas BROWN, James BRIGHTMAN, William BROWN, Thomas BARRY, Anthony BRETON, Thomas BARRY, John BONNER, Peter BOND. Bartholomew CLINCH, Ezekiel CLIFTON, Timothy CAHILL, Charles CHURCHILL, CARMICHAEL. George DAVIS, care of William R. DAVIE, Halifax, John DENNINGTON, James ELLIS. Owen FIELD, William FARRIS, Dr. P. GARVEY, James GILLISPIE, near golden grove, Andrew GREER, Tarborough, the same for Joseph PINE, Frederic GUION, Isaac GUION, Sol. P. GOODRICK, Wake, James GORHAM. Henry HILL, Windsor, John HUMPHRIES, Indian town, Currituck, Edward HALL, Tarborough. Kilby JONES, Bogue, John JOHNSTON. Ambrose KNOX, Alexander DE KIRWAN, Lunsford LONG, Nicholas LONG. His Excellency Alexander MARTIN, John M'RUHON, Mrs. M'ROHON. George ORNS-BY, J. O'BRYEN, Peter ORAM, Peter Butt ORAM. James PARRAT, Notary Public, Daniel PERRY, Philip PALMER, John P. PLEASANT, Joseph PINE. Thomas RHODES, Monsieur RONILHAC, care of William FARRIS, Abraham RATHBURN, Thomas ROGERS, or Silas EMES; John ROUSE, Dobbs county. Doctor John SIBLEY, Fayetteville, Robert & Thomas SNEAD, New River. John Y. THOMPSON, William TUTEN, David TELFAIR, care of Edward HALL(?), Tarborough. George T. VALANCE, Woodstock, John M. VARDIER. John WAL-LACE. Francois X. MARTIN. April 5.

(617) All persons who are indebted to the different concerns in which the late mr. John W. STANLY was interested, as also..to his private estate, will be pleased to make payments... Thomas TURNER. April 13.

(618) The subscriber intending to quit the State requests all persons having demands against him to apply for payment and those indebted to discharge their..accounts. Michael GAILLET. April 15.

(619) Stolen from the subscriber..a handsome black and white Hound Dog... E. PASTEUR. April 15.

(620) William HAWLEY intends leaving this state about the twenty fifth of May next, for a few months... April 15.

(621) John HARVEY, intending to go to Europe on or before the 1st day of June next, desires all persons having demands against him..April 5.

(622) The subscriber has lately removed to the house on the south side of Pollock street, mid-way betwixt Muddy and Eden streets, where he continues to carry on the Watch-Making business.. A Milenary shop is kept in the same house... DE ST. LEGER. April 15.

(623) Newbern, April 15. The Honorable George MASON, Esq. is elected one of the senators of the United States, in behalf of the State of Virginia, in the room of the Hon. William GRAYSON, Esq. deceased.

(624) Married) On Thursday last, Mr. John DEVEREUX to Miss Fanny POLLOCK.

(625) Died) On Tuesday last, in an advanced age, the Rev. Mr. Jacob ABROO, a Jewish Rabbi.

(626) Ten Pounds Reward. Lost, on Sunday the 4th of this present month, between mrs. SIMPSONS and Greenville, a Pocket Book containing ..a note from Moses FIELDS to Samuel GARDNER, for 21 barrels pork.. Thomas WARSON's to Joseph ROSS & co. for 17 pounds and 10 pence.... above reward..to..return the above..to TAGERT ROSS and TAGERT Newbern, Walter HANRAHAN & Co. Washington, Josiah WRIGHT Greensville or the subscribers in Tarborough... Joseph ROSS & Co. Tarborough, April 15.

(627) Caution. All persons are forewarned not to credit or harbour the Crew of the British Ship Caledonia; They are under articles, and I will not pay for them;... James DAVIDSON. April 15.

END OF VOLUME I

ABBOT, ___ 339
  Joseph 131
ABERCROMBIE, ___ 267
ABROO, Jacob 625
ACADEMY, New-Bern 530,571
ACCOCK, Jesse 168
ADAMS, ___ 263
  A. H. 589
  John 116,238,258,341,385,441
  Samuel 116,155,341,472,591
AGNEW, ___ 267,275
AIRY, ___ 423
ALCOCK, William 392
ALDERSON, John 543, 578
  Simon 45
ALDWORTH, Boyle 488
ALEXANDER, Benjamin 204
  Francis 262
ALLEN, ___ 85,195
  Andrew 423
  Eleazer 532
  Ethan 274
  James 423
  John 524
  Sarah 2
ALLSTON, Wm. 516
ALMAND, Moses 489
  Perrin 489
ALMOND, ___ 188
AMHERST, ___ 22
AMIS, Thomas 389
ANDERSON, Bartlett 139
  Benjamin 139
  Garland 139
  Joseph 17
ANDREW, James 43
ANNIBLE, Cornelius 252
ANTHONY, ___ 197
ANTILL, ___ 242
APPLETON, ___ 286
ARANKS, James 403
ARCHER, Edward 610
ARCHIBALD, ___ 271
ARMSTRONG, ___ 254,276
  A. 526
  Andrew 588
ARNOLD, ___ 243

ARNOLD (Cont.)
  B. 243
ASHBURY, Joseph 198
ASHE, ___ 516
  John 108,167,425
  John Baptista 377
  S. 288
  Samuel 309,456
ASTON, ___ 471
ATHERTON, Jeptha 108
AVERY, Leah 332
  W. 408,500
  Waightstill 332,459.
  Waitstill 301,309
AYTON, Philip 229
BA NS, ___ 337
BACON, John 178
BACOT, Peter 229
BAKER, ___ 220
  W. 391
BALLANTINE, Hamilton 323
  James 229
BALLARD, Robert 285
  Thomas 43
  William 575
BANKS, John 168
BANTRAM, Job 125
BARCLAY, John 263
BARKELEY (?), Nelson 139
BARKER, Thomas 466
BARRON, Ann 358
  David 123,174,351,358,368,416,
    427,561
BARROWS, John 497
BARRY, Daniel 365
  John 198,510
  Thomas 616
BARTHOLOMEW, Isaac 490
BATCHELOR, ___ 471
  Edward 81,83,119,200,287,305
  Frances 305,375
BAYLOR, ___ 268,276,505
BAZZEY, James 29
BEACH, T. 158
BEARS, Isaac 124
BEASLEY, John Bap. 481
BEAUFORT, ___ 369
  Gasper 366

BECK, John 191
BECKENHOUT, ___ 477
BECKING, William 612,613
BECKLEY, J. 316
BEDLOCK, James 464
BEE, Thomas 356
BELL, ___ 163
  Caleb 79
  Isaac 403
BENBURY, Thomas 63,108,387
BENEZET, John 96
BENNEHAM, Richard 545
BENNETT, William 91
BENTZ, Pierre 501
BERRY, Charles 58
  Lancelot Crave 58
  Lancelot Grave 117
BIDDLE, ___ 245,257,357
  C. 436
  Edward 68,85
BIGELOW, William 252
BIGGLESTON, James 117,145,164
BILLINGS, Henry 222
BLACK, William 320
BLACKLEDGE, R. 607
  Richard 184,244,266,549,552,
    566,606
  Richard, Jr. 205
BLANCHARD, ___ 583
BLAND, Theo. 262
BLOOMFIELD, Joseph 21
BLOUNT, Benjamin 110
  Jacob 108,266,367,490
  Reading, Jr. 99
  Thomas 490
  William 198,453,459,490,544,
    594
  Wilson 212,368,539,601
BLYTH, Joseph 326,435
BOGART, Nicholas 505
BOHANNON, John 43
BOINOD, ___ 528
BOND, Benjamin 12
  Demsey 89
  Peter 616
BONDFIELD, Charles 91,172,173
BONFIELD, Charles 329
BONNER, Thomas 99,494,616
BOONE, ___ 498
BORBUT, William 43
BORIE, ___ 242
BOUDINOT, Elias 347
BOURDEN, William 517
BOURKE, Thomas 43
BOWERS, Benjamin 113

BOWERS (Cont.)
  Jesse 588
BOWLES, Nath. 29
BOWLY, Daniel 230
BOWMAN, Ebenezer 133
BOYLE, John 43
BRADFORD, Job 161
BRAGGE, John 54
BRAN, Hannah 252
BRANDT, Joseph 237
BRAY, William 217
BRAYAN, William 544
BREHON, James Gloster 577
BRETON, Anthony 616
BREVARD, Eph. 137
BREWTON, Miles 154
BRIDGE, John, Jr. 133
BRIDGES, Robert 8
BRIGHT, James 233
  Simon 233
  Simon, Jr. 108
BRIGHTMAN, James 616
BRIMAGE, W. 289
  William 566
BRINKLEY, Robert 17
BRISSET, Trial 125
BROCK, Joseph 169
BROTHERS, Lory 412,426,470,499,
  501
BROWN, ___ 85,294
  James 133
  John 307,510
  Solomon 127
  Thomas 566,616
  William 108,293,616
BRUIN, ___ 580
BRUSH, ___ 340
BRYAN, Edward 427
  Hardy 367
  J. 359
  John 142,198,232,252,382,538
  John Council 526
  Needham, Jr. 64
  Needham, Sr. 64
  William 64,108,144,208,367,454
  Wm. 260
BRYANT, William 113
BU HANAN, Alexander 513
BUCHANAN, William 179
BUCHANANS, ___ 179
BUCKLAND, ___ 339
BULL, Stephen 154
BULLEY, Robert 158
BUNKER, ___ 269
  Reuben 526

BURGE, Samuel 423
BURGESS, William 49
BURGOYNE, ___ 272,274,278-281,
  298
BURKE, Thomas 108
BURNLY, Hardin 513
BURNSIDE, John 123
BURR, Thaddeus 125
BURRUSS, John 400
BUTLER, John 464
  Zebulon 464
BUTT, Robert 610
BUXTON, Jarvis 198
BYRD, ___ 267
C_BERRITT, Anthony 21
CADWALLADER, ___ 434
CAHILL, Timothy 616
CAKE, Robert 431
CALF, Robert 330
CALVERT, Cornelius 576
CAMBELL, Dugald 459
CAMPBELL, ___ 277,491
  ___habald 4
  Alexander 513
  Archibald 91,174
  Dugald 198
  Duncan 43
  Farquard 108
  James 2,211
  John 108
  William 154
CAPERS, Gabriel 154
CARLYLE, Abraham 506
CARMICHAEL, ___ 616
CARNEY, James 599
CARR___, Joseph 17
CARRAWAY, William 252
CARRINGTON, Edward 279
CARRUTHERS, John 198
CARUTHERS, John 380
CASON, Kelly 380
CASWELL, ___ 327
  Benjamin 388
  H. E. G. 581
  Richard 62,108,227,280,310,328,
    329,349,378,402,475,593
  William 296
CHALKHILL, ___ 2
CHAMBERLAYNE, Byrd 401
  George 401
CHAMBERS, William 43
CHANDLER, John 132
  Samuel 571
CHAPMAN, ___ 85
  Samuel 535

CHAPONEL, J. 574
CHARIOLL, ___ 396
CHARLTON, Jasper 91
CHEEKE, Thomas L. 535
CHEEVER, ___ 77
CHENEY, Abiel 404
CHEW, ___ 276
  Henry 209
CHEYNEY, Philip 198
CHISTIAN, Christopher 48
CHITTENDEN, Thomas 8
CHURCHILL, Charles 616
CLARK, ___ 498
  Abraham 347
  George 198
  Michael 532
  Seth 8
  Thomas 401
CLARKE, Francis 274
  George 43
CLAYTON, Louisa 97
  William 97
CLEAR, ___ 188
  Tim. 50,174,184
CLEMENT, Marc 396
CLIFTON, Ezekiel 616
CLINCH, Bartholomew 616
CLINTON, Geo. 281
  George 315
  H. 281
  Henry 442
CLITHERALL, James 467,479
  John 445,467,479
COART, Joseph 438
COB, Thomas 526
COBB, Jesse 198
COBURN, ___ 263
COCHRAN, John 401
COGDELL, ___ 412,426
  Peggy 264
  R. 252,459,526
  Richard 108,189,198,264,371,
    428,519
COLE, ___ 582,597,611
COLLART, Thomas 218
COLLET, John 164
COLLIER, John 43
  Lockey 515
COLLINS, Hezekiah 55
  John 55
COLLINSON, Thomas 8
CONWAY, ___ 276,434
  Mary 69
COOK, John 321,329,422,566
COOKE, John 233

COOKE (Cont.)
Silas 547
COOMB, ___ 423
___, Jr. 423
COOPER, ___ 168
Gilbert 505
Henry Batts 551
John 551
Samuel 526
COOR, James 57,108,139,144,147,
174,363,544,581
CORD, William 8
CORNELL, ___ 305
Samuel 367,566
CORNWALLIS, ___ 505
CORT, John 198
COTTER, ___ 526
COUPER, John 335
COURT, John 126
COURTNEY, William 419
COUTANCH, ___ 19
COUTER, Herman 401
COWAN, Robert 513
COWPER, John 459
COX, ___ 276
Dan 423,484
Tench 423
CRAFORT, James 43
CRAGHEAD, William 139
CRANE, ___ 491
Benjamin 29
CRAVATH, Lemuel 252
CRAY, William 108
CRESSAP, Michael 166
CRISPIN, Joseph 121
CROGER, ___ 465
CROIG, William 43
CRUDEN, John 398
CRUMP, Goodrich 299
CUNINGHAM, ___ 386
CUNISON, Archibald 179
CUNNINGHAM, ___ 371
CUPPLES, Charles 43
CURTIS, William 1
DABNEY, George, Jr. 139
DADE, Townsend 317
DALY, John 198
Robert P. 500
DALZELL, James 123
DAMES, George 502
DANA, Francis 341
DARK, ___ 277
DAVIDSON, ___ 19
James 627
DAVIE, William R. 616

DAVIE (Cont.)
William Richardson 594
Wm. R. 553
DAVIES, ___ 13
DAVIS, ___ 251,367,496
George 616
James (Page) 1,2,4,7,11
(Item)20,30,31,72,87,108,162,
168,182,185,188,358,373,463,
509
Jonathan 590
Nathan 43
Thomas 565
William 43,252,371
DAWSON, ___ 269
Elizabeth 252
DE BERNOUGH, Galvan 448
DE BRUEL, Michael 43
DE BUTTS, ___ 512
DE HEISTER, ___ 267
DE KIRWAN, Alexander 616
DE LA PORTE, ___ 279
DE ST. LEGER, ___ 622
DEANE, Silas 225, 406
DEBUTTS, John 513
DEKEYSER, Lee 220
DELANCEY, ___ 337
James 338
Oliver 338
DENISON, ___ 464
DENNINGTON, John 616
DENNISON, Nathan 464
DEVENS, ___ 77
DEVEREUX, John 624
DEWEY, ___ 51,437
Stephen 35
DICKENSON, ___ 275
John 85,116
DICKINS, Robert 564
DICKINSON, ___ 268
DICKSON, John 14
DIERANT, Cornelius, Jr. 507
DIGGINS, Peter 418
DIRICKSON, Fulkert 43
DIVIVIER, ___ 405
DIXON, ___ 198,428
Henry 459
William 43
DOBBS, Arthur 15
DOCKERY, Thomas 65
DONALDSON, Samuel 433
DONCASTLE, ___ 139
DOUSE, Joseph 123
DOWTY, Elisha 43
DOYLEY, ___ 357

DRAYTON, William Henry 154
DRY, ___ 532
___ am 533
DUDLEY, Bishop 425
William 595
DUNLAP, ___ 247
DUPLESIS, Manduit 361
DURANT, Cornelius, Jr. 507
DURGEE, Robert 464
DYER, Judath 459
EAGLES, Joseph 537
EARL, Dani__ 63
EASTON, John 526
EATON, Thomas 108
EDES, Benjamin 157
EDMONDS, ___ 85
Thomas 268
EDWARDS, ___ 74
Isaac 205
Mary 587
ELDRIDGE, Zephaniah 194
ELLIOT, Barnard 154
ELLIS, James 616
Richard 45,84,184,190,346,373,
430,463,474,524,593,611
ELLISON, Alderson 150,540
ELMER, Jonathan 347
EMERY, ___ 518
Thomas James 182
EMES, Silas 616
EMMERICK, ___ 337
ETHEREDGE, John 371
ETHEREGE, John 252
ETHERIDGE, ___ 433
EUSTACE, ___ 268
EVERIGIN, Edward 108
EVERITT, Joseph 526
EWEN, William 365
EWING, ___ 85
FALVEY, Michael 562
FARNAN, Matthias 232
FARNSWORTH, Jonas 269
FARR, ___ 334
Richard 27
FARRIS, William 616
FAUNTLEROY, ___ 443
FEBIGER, Christian 602
FENNER, William 459,471
FEREBEE, James 252, 371
FERGUSON, Thomas 154
FERMOY, ___ 276
FIELD, Owen 616
FIELDS, Moses 626
FISCH, ___ 263
FISHER, Henry 478

FISHER (Cont.)
Joseph 28
FITZGERALD, Simon 204
FITZHUGH, Henry 317
FITZPATRICK, James 483
FLEEMING, Sampson 43
FLETT, James 457,458
Katy 457
FLEURY, ___ 491
FLUCKER, Tho. 155
FLY, ___ 339
FONVEILLE, Frederich 87
FONVIELLE, Isaac 117
FONVILLE, Frederick 430
John 358
FORBES, ___ 611
FORBS, David 198
FORD, Joseph 255
FOREMAN, Joseph 43
FOSTER, ___ 125
James 269,318
Thomas 83
FOY, James 462
John 94,136,259
FRANCIS, Ebenezer 221
FRANCK, Edward 332
FRANCKS, Edward 301
FRANKLIN, ___ 350,569
B. 441
Benjamin 76,140,225,406
Temple 569
FRAZER, Jeremiah 108
FREDWEL, John 8
FREEMAN, William 197
FROMENTIER, John Battice 303
FULKERTSON, Fulkert 43
FULMORE, Elizabeth 147
FULSHER, Shadrich 198
GAGE, ___ 22,25,116
Thomas 155
GAILLARD, ___ 528
GAILLET, Michael 618
GAINE, Hugh 300
GALLOWAY, ___ 423,484
Charles 43
James 43
Joseph 85,140
Joseph (?) 68
GANSEVOORT, Peter 243
GARDINER, ___ 77
GARDNER, ___ 124
Samuel 626
GARVEY, P. 616
GASTON, ___ 496,611
Alex. 71,407

GASTON (Cont.)
  Alexander 184,430
GATES,   151,263,272,280,281,
  294,315,337
  Horatio 243,263,274
GATLIN, James 471
GATLING, William 119
GE REL, John 204
  William 204
GEDDY, John 66
GERARD,   472
GERMAN, Joseph 600
GERRY, Eldridge 341,591
GIBBLE, Dederick 526
  Frederick 306
GIDOONWORK, James 401
GILBERT, John 43
GILCHRIST, James 513
  Thomas 546
GILKS, Edward 120
GILLESPIE, Archi___ 534
  Archibald 459
  James 534,616
GILLIARD, John 314
GILLIES, Malcolm 541
GISSARD, Henry 329
GIST, Charles 528
GLASGOW, J. 162,227,280,349,378,
  475
  James 328,329,593
GLOVER,   491
GOAH, Caleb C. 526
GODBY, Cary 8
GOOD, William 198,399
GOODALL, Parke 139
GOODLOE, Robert 107
GORDON, John 43
  Mary 345,413,492
  Patrick 93
GORHAM, James 108,616
GOUGH, Thomas 331
GRA_, D. 560
GRAHAM, James 477
GRANT,   275
  Ebenezer 223
GRANVILLE,   61
  Robert 97
GRAVES, Ann 373
GRAY, Gilbert 371
  Nathan 204
  Thomas 108
GRAYSON, William 623
GREEN,   276,384,491
  Farnifold 367
  J., Jr. 33,228

GREEN (Cont.)
  Jacob 43
  James 198
  James, Jr. 264,322,424
  John 91,266,422,529
GREENAWAY, Benjamin 81
GREENLEAF, Benjamin 158
GREER, Andrew 616
GREGORY, Isaac 108,109
GRIFFEN,   566
GRIMES, Dempsey 113
  James 269
GUERARD,   357
GUION, Frederick 550,616
  Isaac 198,616
GURGANUS, Willie 204
HACKBURN, John 455
HADY, Joseph 252,371
HAGER, Micah 133
HALDIMAND,   55
HALE,   221
HALES, Betty 469
  William 469
HALL, Edward 616
HALL (?),   276
  Edward 616
  Memucan 67
HALLING, Solomon 529,614
HAMILTON, James 43,229
  John 246,271
HAMMOND, Moses 43
HANCOCK, John 77,116,148,155,
  231,243,254,341,342,482
  Joseph 75
HANRAHAN, Walter 626
HARBIN, Robert 28
HARDING, Seth 269
HARDISON, John 34
HARDY,   282
  Ishmael 504
  John 113
  Robert 91
HARE, Moses 98,99
HARGRAVE, Robert 431
HARKENER,   464
HARKER, James 71
HARKIMER,   237
  Johannes Jost 237
HARNETT,   192
  Cornelius 108,387
HARRINGTON, David 132
  John (?) 132
  Levi 135
  Moses, Jr. 132
  Thaddeus 132

HARRIS, John 252
  Robert 41,43
HARRISON, George 437
  Robert H. 254
  Robt. 295
HART, ___ 339
  Thomas 108
HARVEY, Benjamin 108
  Fransina 459
  John 56,62,92,103,108,621
  Thomas 108
HARVY, Matthias 324
HASELL, James 78
HASLEN, ___ 289
  Tho. 118,168
  Thomas 72,87,305
HASTIE, ___ 179
HASTINGS, Samuel 133
HATCH, Edmund 198
  Lemuel 57,108,144
HAWKS, ___ 581
  John 84,117,174
HAWLEY, David 183
  William 620
HAY, Udney 263
HAYNES, Eaton 329
HAZELWOOD, John 284
HAZEN, ___ 242
HEARRING, Jonathan 108,109
HEATH, ___ 77
  Robert 43
  Wm. 405
HENDERSON, ___ 196
  James 257
  John 43
  Robert 43
HENDRICKS, ___ 267,268,276
HENDRICKSON, Salutiel 526
HENLEY, John 53
HENRY, ___ 256
  Patrick, Jr. 139
HERKIMER, ___ 294
HERRITAGE, William 598
  Wm. M. 214
HESLOP, Isaac 513
HEWES, Joseph 61,63,90,91,108
HICKS, Benjamin 236
  Thomas 108
HIDE, Elijah 159
HILL, Green 108
  Henry 616
HILL (?), John 89
HILL, John Horner 458,474
  Thomas 464,608
HINTON, John 108

HOBBS, James 500
HODGE, ___ 583
HODGES, Edward Boucher 379,392
  John, Jr. 610
  Richard 306
HODGSON, Francis 252,371,459,
  471,490
HOELL, Elias 73
HOGG, ___ 477
  Robert 523
HOGUN, J. 391
HOLLINGSWORTH, Jesse 273
HOLT, Josiah 169
HOOPER, George 329
  William 62,108,311
HOPKINS, ___ 339
  George 297
HORTH, ___ 460
HOSMER, ___ 43
HOUSE, ___ 275
  Everitt 201,304,313
  John 252,371
HOUSTON, William C. 239
HOVEY, Seth 70
HOWARD, ___ 414
  John 43
  M. 106,187
  Martin 203,566
HOWE, ___ 161,206,275,307,423
  Robert 108
  William 261,298
HOWSE, Lawrence 447
HUGER, John 154
HUMPHREYS, Charles 68,85
  James, Jr. 298,409
HUMPHRIES; John 616
HUNT, John 288
HUNT, Memucan (See HALL) 108
  Robert 603
HUNTER, ___ 19,198,428
  Thomas 63,108
HUSBANDS, Harman 337
HUSKE, John 523
HUSTON, Andrew 204
HUTCHENS, ___ 25
INDIANS
  Charles 105
  Cheu-Connascon 498
  Dragging Canoe 498
  Rattle-Trap 294
  Turkey's Tail 294
IREDELL, James 309,411
  Jas. 390
IRVIN, James 248
IRVINE, James 241

IRWIN, Henry 43,335
ISLER, John 314
JACKSON, ___ 491
  Thomas 107
JACOBS, John 85
JAMES, Jeremiah 496
  Nicholas 297
JAMESON, ___ 268
JAMIESON, William 43
JARVIS, Samuel 108,109
JASPER (?), Jonathan 42
JAY, John 592
JENKINS, ___ 464
  Benjamin 158
  Hugh 40
  Robert 158
JERDEN, Thomas 595
JOHNSON, Francis 96
  O. B. 125
  Peter 237
  Samuel 593
  Thomas 256
  William 237
JOHNSTON, ___ 16,449
  Amos 43
  Francis 602
  John 108,616
  Samuel 3,53,62,63,108,594
  William 43,526
JOHNSTONE, ___ 473
JONAS, Thomas 91
JONES, ___ 19
  Allen 108,490
  John 41,43
  Joseph 108
  Kilby 616
  Lovick 209
  Samuel 90,104
  Thomas 63,108,195
  Tignal 108
  Willie 108
JOYNER, Laurence 471
JUDGES
  BERRY, Charles 58
JUHAN, James 572
JUSTICES
  BERRY, Lancelot Grave 117
  BONNER, Thomas 494
  DAVIS, James 72,87,182,358,
    373
  ELLIS, Richard 184,373,430,
    463,509,524
  FONVILLE, John 358
  GASTON, Alexander 184,430
  GOODMAN, Henry 126

JUSTICES (Cont.)
  HARE, Moses 98
  HASLEN, Thomas 72,87,165
  HAWKS, John 117
  LEECH, Joseph 165,182,232,524
  ORME, Robert 169
  PATTEN, John 98
  PEARCE, Thomas 99
  RESPESS, Christopher 99
  TISDALE, William 509
  WEBBER, Thomas 169
  WHITE, Robert 126
KANNEIF, Jeremiah 23
KEARSLEY, ___ 275
KEITH, R. 542
  Robert 528
KELLY, Michael 232
KENNAN, William 108
KENNEDY, ___ 25
  John 72,204,232,234,240,392,
    496
  Joseph 137
KENT, William 477
KERN, J. D. 490
KERRY, Gilbert 43
KIDD, Joseph 553
KILL, Thomas 252,371
KINCHEN, John 108,398
KING, Mathew 8
  Richard 43
KNIPHAUSEN, ___ 267
KNOX, Ambrose 616
  Andrew 108
KORNEGE, George 46
  Jacob 46
  John 46
KOWLES, Phillip 600
KUXING, William 43
LA FAYETTE, ___ 254,491
LA PORTE, ___ 448
LAMBERT, John 526
  Mary 20
LANGDON, John 115
LANGWORTHY, Edward 265
LANIER, Burwell 47
  James 108
LANSING, John, Jr. 236
LANSINGH, Jacob J. 263
LAPLANTY, John 303
LAPORTE, Bajieu 449
LAROACH, ___ 229
LASAILRE (?), ___ 448
LATIMER, George 262
LAURENS, ___ 250,491
  Henry 402,415

LAWRENCE, ___ 116
  John 423
  William 611
LAWS, William 532
LAWSON, Elizabeth 558
  William 558
LEACH, Joseph 84
LEATH, Charles 253
LEE, ___ 151,434
  Arthur 406,460
  John 269
  Richard Henry 250,472
LEECH, John 343
  Joseph 108,165,182,232,496,524
  Samuel 43
LEEVINS, Richard 371
LEITH, Charles 312
LENOX, ___ 449
LENT, Cornelia 371
LENTE, Christopher Lewis 613
LESTER, Benjamin 158
  Isaac 158
LEVI, John 477
LILLIBRIDGE, Joseph 43
LINCOLN, B. 161
LISTRE, ___ 459,471
LITTLE, James 198,292
LITTLEJOHN, William 91
LITTLETON, ___ 26
LIVESLY, Thomas 423
LIVINGSTON, ___ 339
  Henry B. 236,491
  Robert 297
  Wil. 451
LIVIUS, Peter 236
LLOYD, Thomas 43
LOCK, Benjamin 132
  Francis 39
  Reuben 132
LOCKEY, Henry 33
LOCKWOOD, James 124
LONG, Lunsford 616
  Nicholas 108,616
LORING, Jonathan 127
LOUDON, ___ 236
LOVEL, ___ 491
LOVELL, James 341
LOVETT, Richard 210
LOVICK, ___ 598
  Anne 214
  George 570
  George P. 259
  George Pheney 214
  George Phiny 468
LOW, Isaac 125,465

LOW (Cont.)
  William 480
LOWRY, ___ 448
  John 207
LOWTHORP, Francis 567
LUTTRILL, John 310
LUX, William 406
LYON, Philip 257
M'CARTHY, Florence 82
M'CAVE, Robert 401
M"CLANAGHAN, Blair 432
M'CLURE, William 571
M'COY, ___ 124
M'CREA, Janey 224
M'CULLOCH, Benjamin 108
M'DOUGALL, ___ 276
M'FARLANE, ___ 125
M'GEHE, Joseph 107
  Mary 107
M'KEEL, John 230
M'KENSIE, Robert 261
M'KINLAY, James 604
M'NICKAL, John 401
M'RUHON, John 616
M'WHAN, William 513
M PHERSON, Alexander 485
MC CLENATKAN, William 43
MC CLURE, ___ 526,541
  John 526
  William 531
MC COY, William 471,490
MC DONALD, Charles 43
MC GUNAY (?), Hugh 40
MC KINNE, William 108
MC KINZIE, Andrew 179
MC KITTRICK, Robert 179
MC KNIGHT, Thomas 235
MC LEAN, John 433
MC LOUN (?), Lackland 43
MC NAIR, ___ 398
MC NIETT, James 43
MAC CORKALL, ___ 19
MAC QUEEN, John 257
MACARTNEY, James 38
MACHEN, H. 596
MACKAY, Patrick 178
MACKENZIE, William 13
MACKNIGHT, Thomas 108,109
MACLEAN, Alexander 145
MADDUX, John 43
MADUIT, ___ 460
MAGOUNE, George 39
MALLERY, John 555
MANLY, J. 602
MARESQUELLE, Louis 216

MARGOLLI, Bernard 476
MARKHAM, John 25
MARSH, Edmund (?) 180
MARSHALL, ___ 477,572
  Joseph 198
MARTIN, ___ 581,583
  Alexander 43,108,262,594,616
  F. X. 602,615
  Francois X. 616
  John 536
  Josiah 44,55,61,94,97,103,145,
    149,164
MASON, George 623
  Zachariah 168
MATTHEWS, ___ 277
MAULE, John 99
MAXWELL, ___ 254,255,258
  Wm. 262
MEAD, Levi 135
MEALS, John 448
MECOY, William 459
MEDICE, ___ 546
MEDLOCK, Charles 65
MEEDS, Abner 133
MEIBORM, ___ 274
MERCER, ___ 25
  Thomas 43
MEREDITH, Joseph 218
MERIDITH, Samuel 139
MIDDLETON, Henry 116
MIFFLIN, ___ 384
  Thomas 68,85,160,602
MILLER, George 108,162
  John 193
  William 43
MILLS, Joshua 532
  William 532
MINOS, James 7
MITCHEL, Thomas 513
MITCHELL, James 122
  John 40
  Mary 43
MITCHELSON, John 12
MONTFORD, Henry 302
  Joseph 302
MONTFORT, Joseph 43,66,108
  Robert 108
MONTGOMERY, ___ 156
MOOR, Andrew 43
  John 557
  William 43
MOORE, ___ 357
  Charles 85
  Joseph 181
  Robert 88,398

MOORE (Cont.)
  Roger 398
  William 204
MORGAN, Charles 217
  Francis 217
MOROW, John 43
MORRIS, ___ 491
  _bert 473
  Anthony 334
  Richard 139
MORTIMER, Charles 512,513
MORTON, John 68,85
MOSELEY, Thomas 377
MOTTE, Isaac 154
MOTTY, James 401
MOULTRIE, William 154
MOUNTFLORENCE, James Cole 588
MOXLEY, ___ 317
MOY, George 113
MOZEY (?), John 133
MUHLENBERG, Frederick Augustus
  592
MUIR, Elizabeth 512,513
  Robert 584
  William 43
MUMFORD, ___ 339
MUNDAY, William 380
MUNROE, John, Jr. 133
  William, III 133
MURE, Robert 584
MURFREE, Hardy 191
MURPHY, Roger 303
MURRAY, Ja. 11
  John 93
N TIE, Isaac 21
NARLCUT, John 526
NASH, ___ 267,268,270,276,277
  A. 101,171,288
  Abner 88,108,141,144,198
  Francis 108,327,353
  Thomas 88
NEALE, Abner 527,593
  Christopher 266
  Philip 403
NEGROES (Incl. Mulattoes)
  Abel Carter 509
  Abraham 72,368,516
  Adam 99
  Ambrose 494
  Ann Driggus 380
  Arthur 39
  Becca 380
  Ben 186,208,210,431
  Billico 169,492
  Billy 165

NEGROES (Cont.)
Bob 182
Boohum 119
Borton 449
Burr 184
Caesar 389
Carolina 330
Cato 143
Charita 380
Charles 126
Charles Fry 545
Charles Thompson 545
Cloe 586
Colas 448
Cork 240
Cudjoe 143
Dick 201,313
Dublin 184
Fan 540
Frank 3
George 79
Grace 87
Hannah 93
Hollow 110
Jack 39,40,98,372,481,595
Jacob 235
Jem 87,117
Joe 527
John 570
John McClish 570
June 143
Kauchee 119
Lewis 358,368
Mayson 143
Nan 517
Peter 42,388,430
Phillis 39
Primus 426,524
Prince 397
Quamino 120
Quash 373
Rachael 39
Rachel 117
Rose 494
Salem 375
Sall 492
Sam 14,209,253
Sarah Blango Moore 494
Scipio 400
Scotland 42
Scrub 545
September 143
Shadrack 380
Shie 48
Smart 188,463,509

NEGROES (Cont.)
Suck 449
Surry 205
Thomas Boman 9
Tom 400
Tom Buck 75
Toney 524
Will 31,234,282,312,313,540
Will Quack 552
York 331
NELSON, Thomas 226
NEUSUM, William 610
NEWTON, Downham 196
NICHOLAS, Robert Carter 139
NICHOLSON, Samuel 420
NILER, Sarah 43
NILES, ___ 339
NORFLEET, Marmaduke 391
Reuben 391
NOTT, Epaphras 372
NOTT (?), Joseph 95
NOY, ___ 124
NUTEN, William 348
O'BRYEN, J. 616
ODAM, Jacob 136,163
OGDEN, ___ 289,364
Phebe 452
T. 439
Thomas 33,405,417,452,493,522,
525,548,585
Titus 333,493,522,525,548,579
OGILVIE, ___ 195
OLDHAM, Thomas 63,108
OLIVER, ___ 488
Joseph 557
ORAM, Peter 616
Peter Butt 616
ORME, Robert 169
ORMES, ___ 371
ORMOND, Roger 108
ORNSBY, George 616
OUTERBRIDGE, Sally 58
OVERTON, Samuel 139
OWENS, John 37,440,525
PAIN, James 43
PAINE, Robert T. 341
PALMER, ___ 245,546
J. 125
Philip 616
Robert 566
William 333
PAMBRUSE, ___ 450
PARK, William 43
PARKER, ___ 128,267,268
Ebenezer 132

PARKER (Cont.)
   J siah 268
   John 129,130
   Jonas 133
PARKHURST, Nathaniel 133
PARRAT, James 289,616
PARRATT, J. 55,78,94,289,616
   James 78,94
PARSON, James 154
PARSONS, Jonathan, Jr. 158
   Samuel H. 337
PASTEUR, E. 619
   William 362
PATRIDGE, Isaac 99,177,330,368,
   446
PATTEN, George 43
   John 96,99,330
PATTERSON, John 513
PATTON, Robert 602
   William 91
PAULET, Peter 471
PAYNE, Michael 593
   Robert Treat 116
PEARCE, Thomas 99
PEARSON,   85
   Tho. W. 111
PEETE, Samuel 43
PEMBERTON, Israel 423
PENDLETON, John 139
PENN, John 108,387,444
PERCY,   112
PERKINS, Solomon 108,109
PERMAIN,   229
PERRY, Daniel 616
PERSON, Thomas 67,108
PETERS, Charles 393
   Richard 602
PETTAWAY (See POTTAWAY), Joseph
   163
PHILIPS,   337
PHIPPS,   125
PICKERING, T. 360
   Timothy 299
PICKETT, William 65
PIERCE, Solomon 133
   William 268
PIERCEY,   124
PILE, William 200
PINCKNEY, Charles 154
PINE, Joseph 616
PINKHAM, Zephaniah 8
PINKNEY,   251
PITCAIRN,   161
PLEASANT, John P. 616
POLK, Thomas 137

POLLIAM (?),   564
POLLOCK, Fanny 624
POLLOK, Cullen 172,173
POSTMASTERS
   COGDELL, R. 252,459,471,526
      Richard 371,490
   MACHEN, H. 596
   MARTIN, F. X. 602
   PATTON, Robert 602
POTTAWAY, Joseph 136
POTTER,   258
POTTS,   263,274,423
POWEL, William 15
POWELL,   279
   Jeremiah 482
   John 371
POWLEY, Izrael 308
POYNER, Nathan 108,109
PRESCOT,   223
PRICE, Paul 12
   Samuel 178
PURDEE, Alexander 428
PURDIE, Alexander 198,495
PURS , Henry 598
PURSS, Henry 568
PUTNAM,   281,315
QUANTOCK,   43
QUINCE, Parker 108
   Richard, Sr. 149
RAMCKE, Frederick 556
RAMS, Henry 64
RAN , Samuel 464
RANDALL, William 198
RANDEL, William 500
RANDOLPH,   560
   Peyton 116,138,140
RANSOM, James 108
RATHBURN, Abraham 616
RAWLINS, James 232
READING, Joseph 108
REASONOVER, Joseph 586
REED, James 518
   Joseph 96,473
   Joshua 132
   Joshua, Jr. 132
   Nathan 132
REILLY, Phillip 562,563
REMER, Thomas 21
RESPESS, Christopher 99
RESPISS, Thomas, Jr. 108
REW, Southy 12
RHOADS, Samuel 68
RHODES, Henry 108
   Thomas 616
RICE,   16,183

RICE (Cont.)
John 16,234
RICHARDSON, ___ 19
Dorothy 86
George 29
John 118
RIDING, Benjamin 526
RIEBEUR (?), Peter 21
RIGGS, John 282,313
RILEY, ___ 339
RIVINGTON, James 300
ROBERTS, Owen 154
ROBERTSON, James 395
ROBI___, William 89
ROBINS, John 130
ROBINSON, Charles 65
John 98,139,204
William 113
ROBSON, William 108
ROCHESTER, Nath 419
ROGERS, ___ 25
Joseph 555
Michael 108
Miriam 555
Thomas 616
ROMBOUGH, John 91
RONILHAC, ___ 616
ROOKE, Bartholomew 102
ROSE, Alexander 178
ROSS, ___ 597
George 68,85
James 21,421
Joseph 626
ROUSE, John 616
ROWA__, John 533
ROWAN, John 108
Matt. 11
Robert 108,397
ROWLAND, Andrew 125
RUDDIMAN, Tho. 461
RUMSEY, James 560
RUSEL, Philip 132
RUTHERFORD, Griffith 108
RUTHERFURD, Thomas 108
RUTLEDGE, Hugh 355
John 354-356
SAGG, George 371
SALTER, Edward 108,152,381
SAMUEL, ___ 477
SANDEFUR, Thomas 447
SANDERS, ___ 492
SANDERSON, Elijah 127
SARRAZIN, ___ 357
SATHERTHWAITE, William 204
SAUNDERS, John 229

SAUNDERSON, Samuel 133
SAVAGE, ___ 454
Thomas 154
SCAMMELL, Alexander 383
SCATER, Hugh 215
SCHOMBERG, J. 521
SCHUYLER, ___ 236,294
Hanjort 243
Philip 151,231
SCOT, Nathaniel 8
SCOTT, ___ 268,277,335
SCUDDER, Nathaniel 347
SEARS, ___ 277
SEVIER, John 605
SHARP, William 108
SHAW, Robert 198
SHAWICK, ___ 526
SHELTON, Meriwether 139
SHEPHERD, ___ 306
John 328
Solomon 108
SHERIFFS
BRYAN, J. 359
John 142,232,496
HOVEY, Seth 70
KENNEDY, John (Dep.) 496
LOCKEY, Henry 33
REW, Southy 12
SKINNER, Evan 235
WILLIAMS, Lewis 36
SHERMAN, Christopher 204
SHIPPEN, ___ 275
SHOEMAKER, ___ 423
SHORE, Thomas 386
SHORT, Robert 29
SIBLEY, John 616
SILBY, Barridge Hutchins 70
SIMONDS (?), Joseph 132
SIMONS, Lewis 303
SIMPSON, ___ 306,626
John 108,152,606,607
SINCLAIR, ___ 376
SINGLETARY, Alevy 526
SINGLETON, Spyers 266,544
SITGREAVES, John 530,531,571,604
Thomas 410
SKINNER, ___ 41
Evan 235
SKISKER, ___ 317
SLADE, Elijah 204
SMALLWOOD, ___ 242,258,276,580
SMITH, ___ 498,559
Benjamin 532,533
Deborah 374
John 14,64,514,526,554,573

SMITH (Cont.)
  Jonathan B. 96
  Joseph 401
  Matthew 268
  Nathan 587
  Phineas 132
  Robert 91
  Samuel 42,114
  Samuel, Jr. 64
  Samuel, Sr. 64
  Thomas 357
  Timothy 134
  William 423
SNEAD, Robert 616
  Thomas 616
SPAIGHT, R. D. 581
  Richard 18
  Richard Dobbs 50,594,611
  William 252
SPEIGHTS (?), ___ 74
SPENCER, Sam. 520
  Samuel 65,309
SPICER, John 371
SPIGHT, William 480
SPOTIWO D, ___ 277
SPROTT, Thomas 326
SPRUIL, Benjamin 108
  Joseph 108
ST. CLAIR, Ar. 247
STAFFORD, Elisha 394
STANDLEY, David 108
STANLEY, John W. 336,493
STANLY, J. W. 439
  John W. 245,286,507,617
  W. 146
STANTON, Henry 219
  Hope 219
STANWIX, ___ 25
STARK, ___ 294
STARKEY, Edward 108,585
  John 417
  Peter 516
  Phebe 417
START, ___ 339
STEADMAN, Ben 393
STEARNS, ___ 132
STEDMAN, Ben. 293
  Benjamin 204
STEEL, John 459
STELE, Richard 379
STEPHENS, ___ 19
STEVENSON, ___ 582,597,611
  Ann 609
  Silas 527
STEWART, ___ 465

STEWART (Cont.)
  Alex. 165
  David 230
  John 242
STIMPSON, Stephen 252,371
STITH, ___ 317
STOBO, Robert 24
STONE, ___ 267,268,276
  Usebious 391
STORMONT, ___ 225
STORY, Enoch 423
STOW, ___ 215
STRINGER, ___ 423
STROBHAR (?), John 143
STURGIS, Jonathan 125
SULLIVAN, ___ 242,267,276
  John 115,236,247,486,491
SUMNER, James 90,104
  Luke 90
SURLING, ___ 276
SYME, John 139
TABB, William 105,175
TAGERT, ___ 597,626
TALBOT, ___ 491
TAVERNER, ___ 158
TAVERNOR, George 120
TAYLOR, ___ 297
  Edmund 186
  Joseph 329
  William 186
TAZEWELL, John 316
TELFAIR, David 616
TELLFAIR, William 477
TEMPLE, John 477
  William 526
TERRY, Partial 464
THALLEY, John 532
THARP, Job 371
THOMAS, Billy 79
  William 65
THOMLINSON, ___ 393
THOMPSON, ___ 85
  Charles 140
  John Y. 616
  William 108
THOMSON, Balaam 325
  Charles 127,148,202,206,213,
    243,249,250,254,283,315,327,
    415,429,441
  David 201,290,313
TIDD, Benjamin 131
  Samuel 132
  William 132
TIER, Richard 566
TIMOTHY, Peter 154

TINKER, Jehiel 459,471
TISDALE, ___ 232
  William 463,496,509
TODD, Joseph 555
  Mallery 555
TOOL, Henry Irwin 335
TOOMER, Hen. 311
TOPPING, William 204
TOWLES, ___ 277
TOWZER, Charles 380
TRAVERS, Patrick 59
TRENT, Alexander 512,513
TRIGG, ___ 21
TRUMBULL, Joseph 213
TRUSTER, ___ 19
TRUXTON, ___ 569
TRYON, ___ 205
  William 32,337
TUCKER, ___ 336
TULLY, Anthony 204
  Henry 204
TUNNO, ___ 477
TURNER, John 371
  Thomas 290,617
TUTEN, William 616
TUTON, Oliver 563
TYSON, John 113,176
VAIL, ___ 360
  Edward 90
VALANCE, George T. 616
VALKENBURGH, J. V. 236
VAN DAM, Rip 21
VAN DYCK, ___ 236
VAN TASSEL, Cornelius 337
  Peter 337
VAN VEIGHTEN, ___ 224
VANCISE, ___ 526
VARDIER, John M. 616
VARNUM, ___ 491
VERRIER, James 80
VILES (?), Joel 132
VIPON, Henry 165,246
VISSCHER, Matt. 263
VOLANTE, Andero Grimalde 5
WADE, ___ 491
  Thomas 65
WADSWORTH, ___ 124
WAITE, William 564
WALCOTT, ___ 267
WALKER, Richard 28
WALLACE, ___ 19
  Elizabeth 376
  Hugh 156
  John 616
WALLINGTON, Enoch 132

WANE, ___ 258
WARBURTON, ___ 344
WARD, ___ 151
  Sam. 285
  William 64
WARNER, ___ 294
WARREN, James 591
WARSON, Thomas 626
WARWICK, ___ 208
WASHINGTON, ___ 151,160,206,236,
  256,258,270,284,288,299,360,
  361,442,486,602
  Elizabeth 459
  G. 202,254
  George 295,560
  Thacker 317
WATSON, William 204,393
WATTS, Stephen 237
WAYNE, ___ 85,254,276
WEBB, ___ 339
  James 610
  John 66,108
WEBBER, Thomas 169
WEEKS, ___ 401
WEISS, ___ 334
WELLS, Samuel 178
WENDELL, John W. 236
WEST, ___ 339,566
  George 204
  Robert, Jr. 9
  Robert, Sr. 9
WESTCOTE, Robert 29
WESTMORE, ___ 454
WHEDBEE, John, Jr. 108
WHILTBANK, Abraham 511
WHITAKER, Benjamin 74
WHITE, ___ 77
  Ebenezer 8
  Jack 276
  John 291
  Paul 153
  Robert 126
WHITEFIELD, George 6
WHITLY, Joseph 421
  Thomas 421
WHITNEY, ___ 526
WHITTY, Edward 198
WILKINSON, James 263
  Thomas 204
  William 186,192
WILLIAMS, ___ 274
  Ben 606,607
  Benjamin 64,526
  E. B. 125
  Edmund 113

WILLIAMS (Cont.)
  John 113,186,387,414,594
  Joseph 532
  Lewis 36,440
  Nath. B. 440
  Robert 37,52,108,414
  Thos. 570
  William 401
WILLIAMSON, Francis 108
WILLING, ___ 307
  Thomas 140
WILLIS, A. 611
  Mildred 577
WILSON, ___ 25
WINSHIP, John 133
  Simon 128
  Thomas 132
WINSON, ___ 566
WITHERSPOON, John 347
WO FLEY, ___ 366
WOLFE, ___ 22,25
WOLFENDEN, George 508
WOLGAN, Tho. 43
WOOD, ___ 560
  Joseph 265
  Margaret 503
  William 503
WOODBURY, John 234
WOODFORD, ___ 254
WOOLCUTT, W. 29
WORSLEY, Joseph 487
WORTH, Joseph 108
WRENFORD, ___ 290,507
  Edmond 291,352
  Edmund 69,170
WRIGHT, John 418
  Joseph 95
  Josiah 626
  Micahel 95
WYMAN, James 132
WYNNS, George 108
YARD, ___ 275
YATES, ___ 263
YEATS, Daniel 490
YOUNG, Henry 120

BANKS, Blue 532,533
  Red 508
BAR, Occacock 54,328
BOGUE 579,616
BRANCH, Popular 566
BRIDGE, Peacock's 168,191
  South-West 14
  Trent 603
CAPE, Fear 88,398
  Hatteras 336
CITY
  Boston 7,27,29,77,80,112,122,
    125,129,155,157,161,194,216,
    221,238,269,340,341,420,482,
    491,504,510,591
  New-York 21-23,29,115,125,156,
    158,242,315,338-340,434,442,
    465,477,485,505,560,569,575
  Philadelphia 6,21,25,29,60,62,
    68,80,85,96,108,115,116,124,
    159,166,193,206,225,231,238,
    241,242,247,248,254,255,256,
    275,298,307,366,395,409,423,
    432,441,442,444,472,473,478,
    483,484,491,506,510,528,529,
    569,584,592,602
CREEK
  Adam's 121
  Bachelor's 522
  Batchelor's 601
  Beaver 74
  Black 219,414
  Brandywine 254,255
  Brice's 71,289,489,566
  Broad 119,380
  Clubfoot's 43,209,210
  Contentny 168
  Coor 260
  Cross 479
  Dawson's 111
  Durham's 165
  Fish 278
  Fishing 447
  Fork 53
  Gardner's 34
  Goose 566

CREEK (Cont.)
  Great Contentney 201,306
  Green's 380
  Holly Shelter 368
  Hyco, Double Creeks of 564
  Lynch's 53
  Moses's 224
  Mosley's 566
  Mountain 53
  Oneida 464
  Otter 259
  Piercey's 74
  Richland 590
  Rock-Fish 2,377
  Slocomb's 30,188
  Smith's 21,74,526
  Swift's 252,538
  Town 566
FERRY, Cox's 459
  Everard's 2
  Kemp's 601
FLATS, German 243
FORD, Chad's 254
  Old 418
  Swede's 258
FORGE, Valley 258,383,442
FORK, Tillers 53
FORT
  Chartres 498
  Daton 243
  Exeter 464
  Independence 315
  Montgomery 339
  Schuyler 243,294
  Stanwix 237,464
  Ticonderoga 236,250,263
HILL
  Bunker 157
  Bunkers 112
  Cheraw 520
  Winter 124
  Winter's 159
HOOK, Sandy 156,434
INLET, Bogue 405,459
ISLAND
  Eagle's 537

ISLAND (Cont.)
Long 339
Occacock 49
Sapello 178
Staten 242
LAKE, Ellis's 289,566
MEADOWS, Tuckahoe 390
NECK, Charlestown 157
Northern 317
PENGO 578
PLANTATION
Eden-House 10
Forks 537
Golden Grove 616
Green Spring 30,188,463,509
Hamlet 52
Lilleput 2
Milton 601
Pembroke 101
Sportsmans-Hall 557
Springfield 2,330,446
POINT
Crown 22,25
Elizabeth Town 242
Rockey 2
Rocky 93,377
Union 81,83
PUNGO 595
RIVER
Bay 282,393
Cape-Fear 47,53,377
Charles 112,157
Dan 43
James 320,386
Mississippi 25,498
Mohawk 243
Neuse 21,51,74,259,289,306,
380,403,414,471,479,526,554,
566,570,587,601
New 2,36,371,440,447,459,532,
616
New-Port 244
North 315
North-East 2,516
Ohio 166,498
Pamplico 208
Pamptico 566
Pee Dee 53,229
Pungo 372
Roanoke 34,234
Schuylkill 258
Sinepuxent 194,432
South 509
Susquehannah 464
Tar 459

RIVER (Cont.)
Tarr 306
Trent 84,101,171,259,371,390,
479,490,557
York 122
ROAD
Hampton 512,513
Neuse 170
Trent 74,170
ROCK, White 408
SAVANNAH, Miry 566
SETTLEMENT, Wyoming 464
SHELL, Mussele 394
SOUND, Bogue 52
Core 71,184,244,414,463,479
SQUARE, Ellis's 100
SWAMP
Maxwell's 2,532
Nauhunte 306
Soracte (?) 2
Wheat 306
TOWN
Albany 22,24,237,263,278
Alexandria 194,512
Amboy 202,242
Amesbury 575
Annapolis 275,406
Baltimore 256,258,261,276,315,
334,348,384,406,423,443,473,
478,497,506,560
Bath 540,546,566
Beaufort 27,33,52,79,219,244,
289,312,404,414,459,470,476,
479,490,501,526,600
Brandford 125
Bridgewater 216
Brookline 125
Brunswick 2,19,108,202,479
Burlington 347
Cambridge 112,125,155
Campbelton 108,397
Canterbury 125
Castle Town 221
Charles-Town 19,25,26
Charlestown 112,154,157,159,
161,178,195,217,229,245,257,
354,357
Charlotte 137
Chester 254,255,483
Chesterfield 320
Concord 112,125,127,129
Cortlandts 263
Deep Creek 179
Dunant 414
E. Guilford 125

TOWN (Cont.)
East Bradford 334
East Windsor 223
Edenton 53,63,88,91,108,172,
  173,195,235,329,350,376,411,
  433,434,448,450,454,481
Elk 273
Eriskie 237
Fairfield 125
Fayetteville 590,616
Fish-Kill 183,224,236,297,337,
  505
Frederick 166
Fredericksburg 138,363,448,512
George Town 19
Georgetown 234,372
German 267,270,276,299,318,327,
  353,360,423
Greensville 626
Greenwich 338
Guilford 125
Halifax 35,66,108,179,246,289,
  302,324,329,393,546,553,588,
  616
Hallifax 53
Hampton 19
Hanover 236
Hartford 124,223
Haverford 334
Hillsborough 108,302,325,329,
  398,419,526,553
Hingham 161
Hugbarton 221
Hurley 297
Indian Town 616
Killingsworth 125
Kingston 238,263,296,306,464,
  526
Kinsbridge 315,337
Lancaster 263,294,303
Lebanon 159
Lewis-Town 478,511
Lexington 124,125,127-135
Lincoln 131
Lixington 112
Louisburg 588
Lyme 125
Manchester 221
Maroneck 337
Martinborough 289,335
Martinsborough 152
Minotamy 112
Monmouth 442
Morristown 242
New haven 125,183

TOWN (Cont.)
New-Garden 526
New-London 125,222,339
New-Port 559
New-Windsor 281
Newbern 2,14-16,18,63,71,73,78,
  80,92,94,100,101,106,108,119,
  121,123,124,144,147,162,170,
  174,188,189,201,205,207,211,
  212,214,215,229,230,234,246,
  251,252,260,264,266,286,287,
  289-292,310,311,313,314,322,
  326,329,330,333,336,345,346,
  351,352,359,362-365,368,371,
  373-375,379,380,382,387,390-
  393,399,403,405,408,410,413,
  414,416,417,424,427,428,436-
  438,440,448,452,453,475-459,
  463,466,471,475,479,488,490,
  492,493,496,499,501,518,519,
  522,524-532,535,536,539,541,
  542,544,547,548,550,554,556-
  558,561,565-568,570-573,581-
  583,585,587,596,602,603,605,
  606,611,613,616,623,626
Newbury Port 158,269
Newcastle 139
Newport 112
Norfolk 19,576,610
Norwich 125
Old Tappa 505
Orange 179
Oswego 22
Perkiomy 299
Petersburg 179,386
Pittsburgh 25
Plainfield 125
Port-Beaufort 8
Portsmouth 420,584
Potowmack 317
Poughkeepsie 464
Poupon 19
Prince-Town 347
Providence 21,125,193,559
Purrysburgh (?) 143
Quibble 202
Red-Bank 284,285
Rhynebeck 297
Richlands 440
Salisbury 108,136,163,329
Saratoga 274,299
Savannah 19
Saybrook 125
Shetocket 339
Skippack 268

TOWN (Cont.)
  South Bay 221
  Southold 339
  Stillwater 263
  Stratford 183
  Suffolk 19
  Swansborough 523
  Tarborough 43,181,335,447,563,
    590,593,594,616,626
  Titticut 216
  Tiverton 491
  Trenton 275,451,586
  Urbanna 421
  Wallingford 124
  Warner 575
  Warrenton 577,588,590
  Washington 335,549,563,626
  Watertown 125,157
  White Marsh 360
  White Plains 484,486
  Williamsburg 19,122,138,226,
    256,277,279,307,316-318,386,
    432,447,460,495,498,511
  Wilmington 2,13,53,108,120,149,
    186,192,215,218,220,273,311,
    329,397,400,425,523,537,551-
    553,562,596,608
  Windsor 179,616
  Woodstock 75,125,372,502,546,
    616
  Worcester 125
  Yorktown 207,226,267,268,294,
    307,318,395,402,406,409
TOWNSHIPS
  Exeter 464
  Huntington 464
  Kingston 464
  Lackewana 464
  Nanticoak 464
  Plymouth 464
  Salem 464
  Wilkesborough 464